MW01635506

NATURE LOVER'S GUIDE

SCOTT WEIDENSAUL

NATURE LOVER'S GUIDE

SCOTT WEIDENSAUL

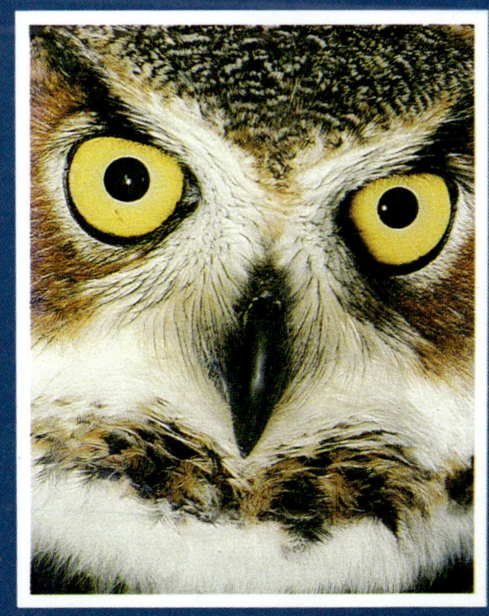

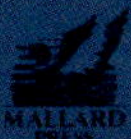

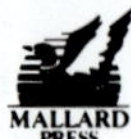

MALLARD PRESS

An imprint of BDD Promotional
Book Company, Inc.,
666 Fifth Avenue
New York, N.Y. 10103

Mallard Press and its accompanying logo are trademarks of BDD Promotional Book Company, Inc.

First published in the United States of America in 1991 by the Mallard Press

ISBN 0-792-45353-0

A QUINTET BOOK

This book was designed and produced by
Quintet Publishing Limited
6 Blundell Street
London N7 9BH

Creative Director: Peter Bridgewater
Art Director: Ian Hunt
Designer: Stuart Walden
Project Editor: Caroline Beattie
Artwork: Danny McBride

Typeset in Great Britain by
Central Southern Typesetters, Eastbourne
Manufactured in Hong Kong by
Regent Publishing Services Limited
Printed in Hong Kong by
Leefung-Asco Printers Limited

PICTURE CREDITS

The Publishers would like to thank the following for supplying the illustrations for this book:

Tom Fegely: pages 26, 27, 28 (top) and 48 (top).

Kerry A. Grim: pages 16 (bottom) and 56 (top).

Carl A. Hess: page 21.

Marcus Schneck: pages 10, 38 (top) and 39 (left).

Scott Weidensaul: pages 6, 7, 8, 9, 11, 12, 13,14, 15, 16 (top), 17, 18, 19, 20, 22, 23, 24, 25, 28 (bottom), 29, 30, 31, 32, 33, 34, 35, 36, 37, 38 (bottom), 39 (right), 40, 41, 44, 45, 46, 47, 48 (bottom), 49, 50, 51, 52, 53, 54, 55, 56 (bottom), 57, 58, 59, 60, 61, 62, 63, 64, 65, 66, 67, 69, 70, 71, 72, 73, 74, 75, 76 and 77. The line art on pages 42 and 78 was drawn by Vana Haggerty, adapted from *Woodworking for Wildlife*, with permission from Pennsylvania Wild Resource Conservation Fund.

Contents

CHAPTER ONE

Introduction

THIS BOOK IS AN explorer's manual, you might say, for people who enjoy the outdoors and want to learn more about it.

With the rise in environmental concern, studying natural history has never been more popular. Visitation to parks and refuges is at all-time highs, but you needn't travel far to enjoy the outdoors. A fascinating world lies just beyond your back door – a world that encompasses all the complexities of the environment as a whole.

As science learns more about the way the planet functions, we are coming to recognize the staggering interdependencies between plants, animals – and humans. No living thing exists in a vacuum – all are inexorably linked through bonds of food, shelter, migration and a thousand other connections both obvious and subtle. The bear and the butterfly, the whale and the deer and the person, all depend on the same fundamental systems.

Even amateur study quickly makes clear that nothing in nature is simple. Take a stream flowing down a hill, a creek so small it can be spanned by a single hop. Within its narrow confines exists a food chain of bewildering complexity. Microscopic plankton and algae convert the energy of sunlight, water and nutrients to food. They are fed upon by herbivorous insects – mayflies, midge larvae, water pennies, caddisflies and others. They, in turn, are preyed upon by stonefly larvae, water beetles, small fish and other meat-eaters. Within a short stretch of creek there may be hundreds, sometimes thousands, of different organisms – not to mention the overlap between terrestrial and aquatic food chains, like the kingfisher that plunges beneath the water and comes up with a dace.

Perhaps the most important benefit of nature study is an appreciation for, and concern about, the fragility of the environment, in which a single thoughtless act can have wide-ranging effects. *The Nature Lover's Guide* offers an alternative to the old-fashioned "collect it and stuff it" approach to outdoor learning. The dozens of hands-on activities and explorations that follow will increase awareness and understanding, without leaving a trail of death and destruction in your wake. Special sections on materials and techniques give even the beginner the foundation on which to start learning, and a section on advanced techniques points the

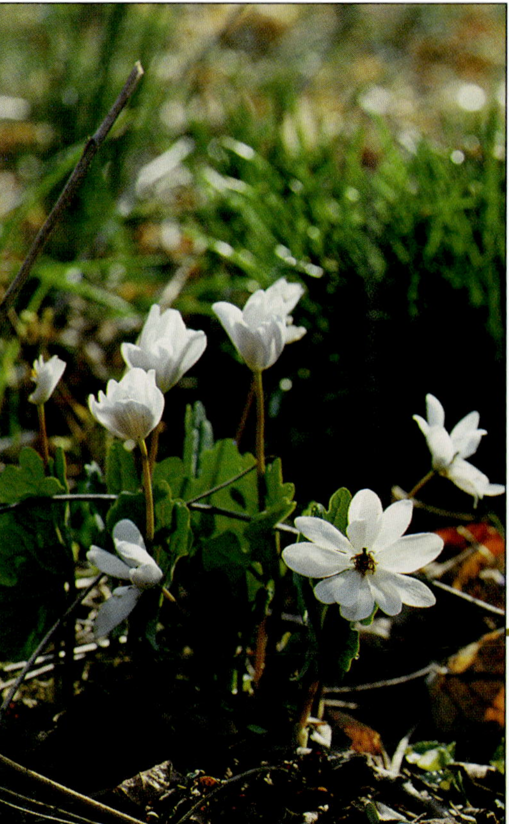

RIGHT A clump of bloodroot, pushing through dead leaves and into the April sun, is just one link in a vast, complex web that binds all living things.

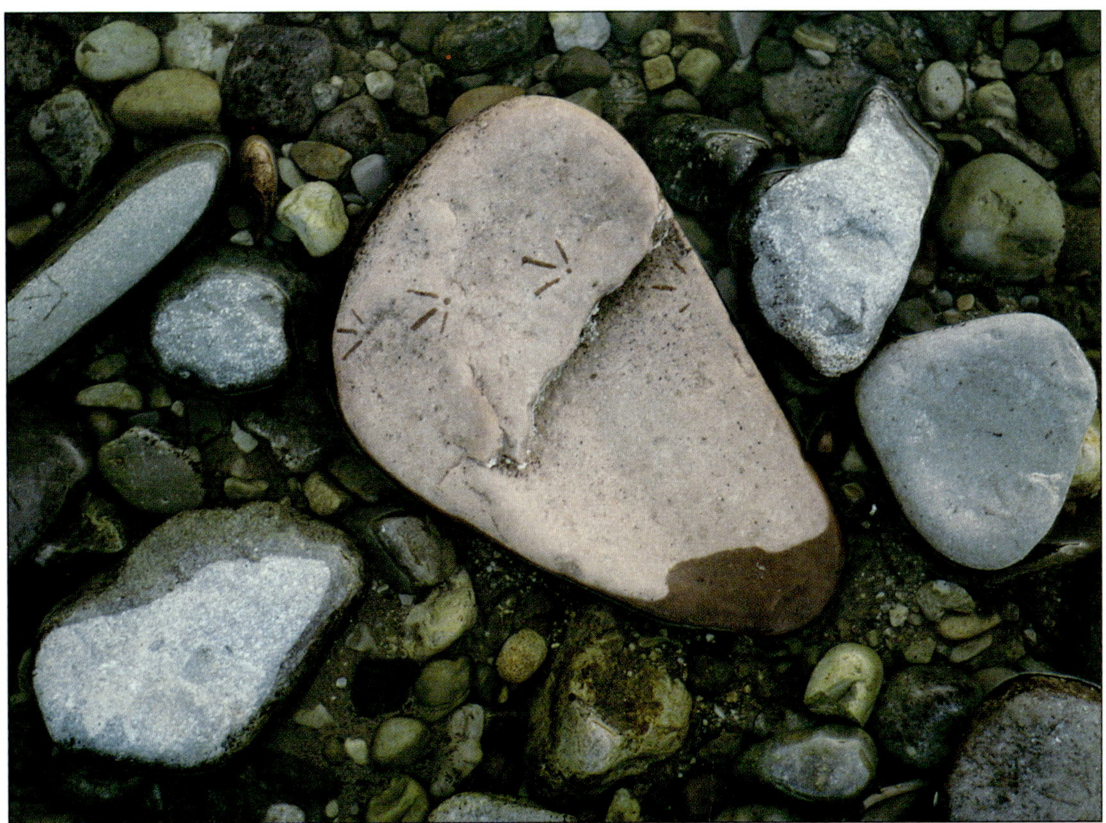

LEFT Wet footprints on river rocks are the mute record of a spotted sandpiper's visit, but to the observant naturalist they speak volumes.

more experienced naturalist in new directions.

At one time, nature study generally meant amassing large collections of dead plants and animals, neatly pressed between the pages of herbariums, pinned in glass cases or stuffed and lifeless in drawers. But today, the emphasis – refreshingly – is on non-intrusive methods of study that respect the subject. While many of the activities in this book describe ways to capture living creatures for study, the animal's well-being should always be the major consideration. In those cases where dead specimens are required (such as for study skins or skull collections), it is important to salvage animals already dead. Granted, the removal of a few insects or mice for a collection will have a negligible biological impact on the environment as a whole, but it has a far greater impact on our sense of stewardship for the outdoors. By treating every part of the ecosystem with care, we develop a deeper respect for the whole.

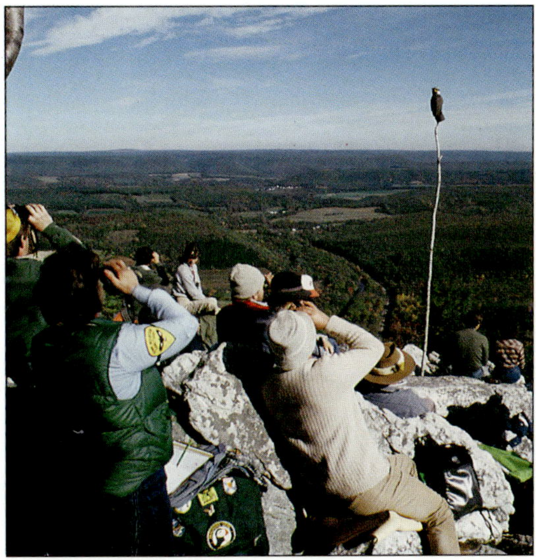

LEFT Never before has outdoor recreation and environmental study been as popular as it is today.

Most of all, remember that nature study should be fun, infused with a sense of discovery – a thrill you'll feel the first time you watch a silk moth emerge from its cocoon, see a meteor flame across the sky, or discover a long-hidden fossil. Good luck, and enjoy!

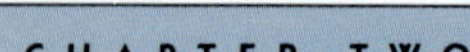

CHAPTER TWO

Materials and Field Techniques

CHOOSING AND USING EQUIPMENT

HAND LENS

THE CHEAPEST, YET MOST useful piece of equipment any naturalist can own is a hand lens – nothing more than a small magnifying glass, usually with a case into which the lens folds for protection. Plastic hand lenses can be had for a dollar or two, but they scratch easily and rarely offer quality magnification, so invest a few dollars more and buy a good quality glass lens with metal fittings. It will last a lifetime.

Hand lenses open up an unseen world right at your fingertips – a world of tiny insects, minute plants, hidden details. Through a hand lens you can watch a new-born caterpillar chew its way out of its egg, or examine the threadlike veins in the fossil of a fern. Once you get in the habit of using a hand lens, you'll never go afield without one again.

If you should find yourself without a hand lens, though, your binoculars can

BELOW Binoculars are simply essential for watching most birds and mammals. While many different magnification rates are available, seven-power binoculars are best for general wildlife viewing.

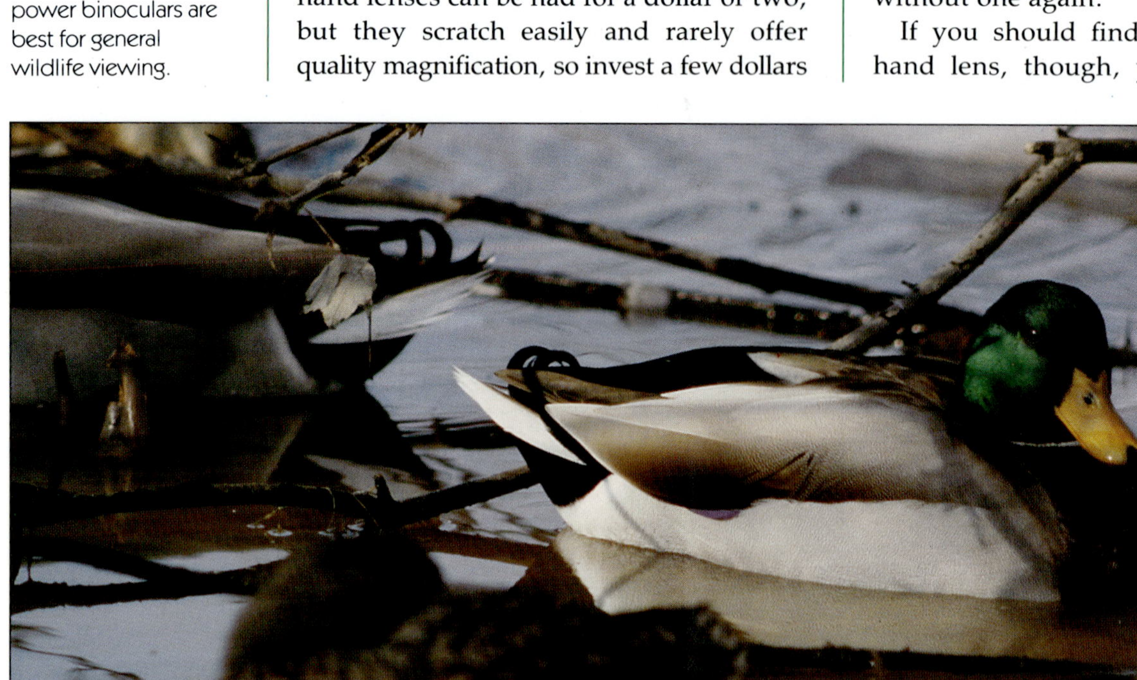

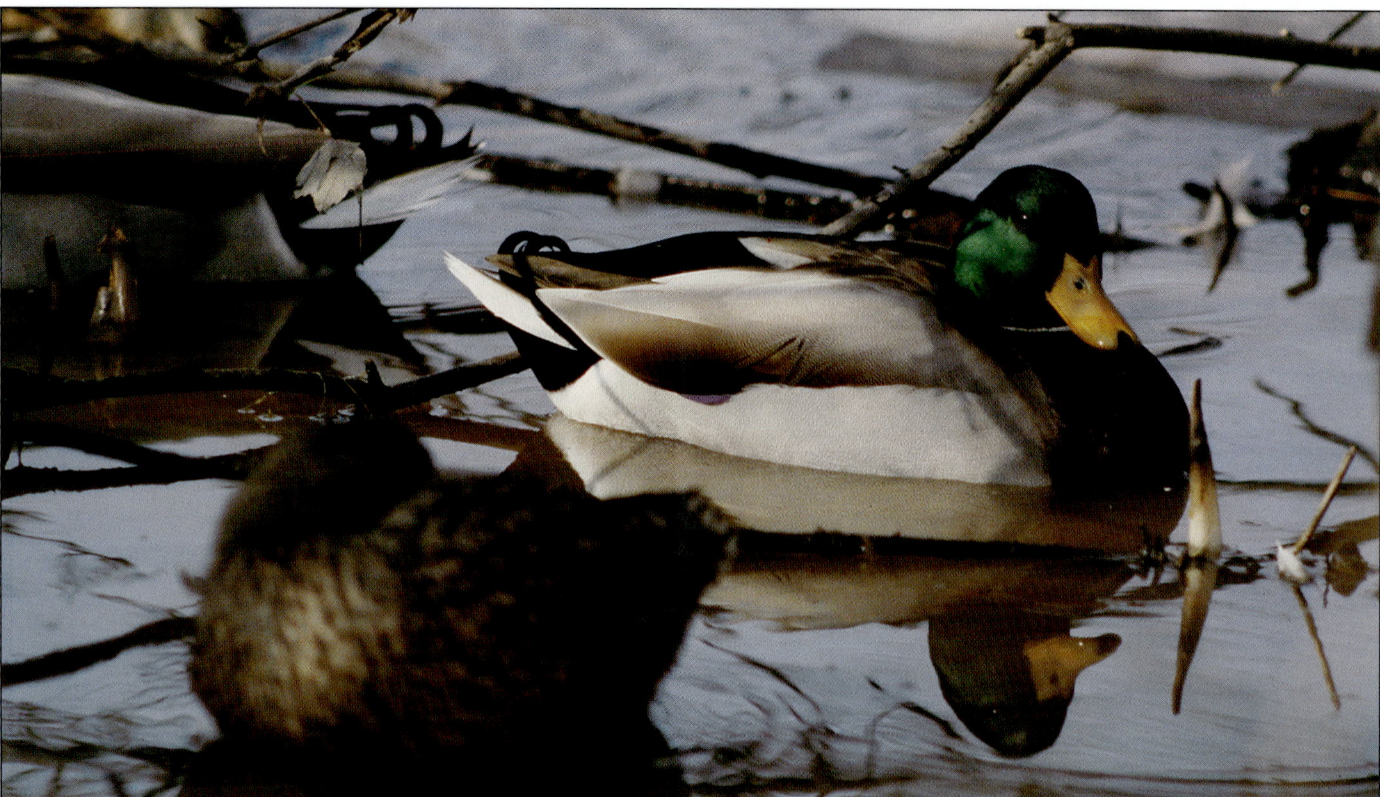

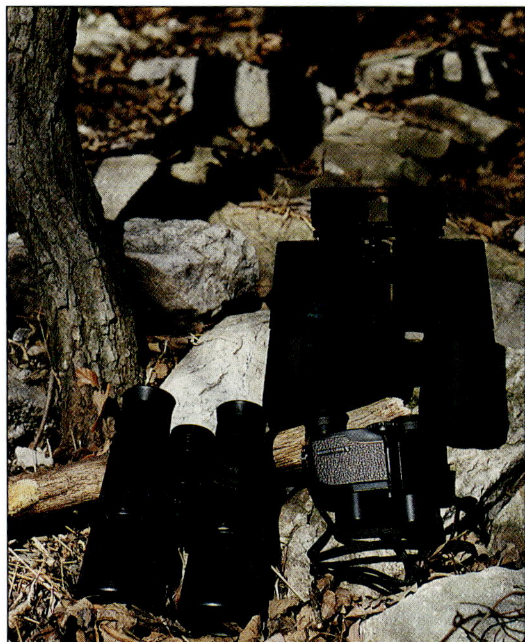

serve in a pinch. Reverse them, and hold one of the large objective lenses near your eye while placing the other end near the object of interest. The binoculars give a somewhat distorted, fish-eye effect, but it works when nothing else is available.

BINOCULARS

Binoculars are essential for observing birds and mammals, but there are many styles and variations, each suited to a particular purpose.

The most important consideration is magnification. Binoculars come in differing magnifications and with differing fields of view, both expressed by numbers. The most common combination is 7x35; the first refers to the magnification, in this case seven power, and the second is diameter of the objective (or large) lens in millimeters, which determines how big an area is visible. Obviously, a pair of 10x40 binoculars will give greater magnification and field of view than a set of compact 7x25 glasses. For general birding and wildlife viewing, 7x35 binoculars are the best all-around choice.

For watching distant animals, like migrating hawks, higher magnification is called for, either 8 or 10 power; such glasses usually come with a wider field of view (from 40 to 50) to compensate for the greater strength. Compact binoculars are becoming increasingly popular, although their reduced power and field of view make them primarily back-up glasses to be carried when a larger pair would get in the way.

SPOTTING SCOPES

There are times when binoculars simply do not give enough magnification. In such situations, a spotting scope is the answer.

Spotting scopes are terrestrial telescopes designed for mid-range magnification, anywhere from 15 power up to 60 or 70 power. Although they are valuable for watching mammals, scopes are used most often by birders for observing distant birds – shorebirds on a tidal flat, or flocks of ducks beyond the surf line, for instance. They are also good for long-term observations, like those at a nest.

The most common models are refractor (prismatic) scopes, which are also the least expensive – although that is a relative term, and an average refractor spotting scope will cost several hundred dollars. Most offer zoom capability, usually from about 15–45x, sometimes as high as 60x. In practical terms, however, the best viewing through a zoom scope is at the lower end of the power scale; at high magnification the image will become darker and fuzzier.

Catadioptric – or "cat" – scopes use mirrors to compress higher magnification into a reasonably small package. Much more expensive than refractor scopes, cats are also much heavier, and usually show a reversed image – all reasons for their lower popularity among naturalists.

Any scope requires support of some sort. A tripod is the best, but is bulky to carry in the field. For light refractor scopes, try mounting the lens on a wooden gunstock, carried slung on a shoulder strap. When viewing, brace your arms against a tree or rock to steady yourself.

LEFT Binoculars come in three styles – the standard porro prism binoculars with offset eye-pieces (top); compact binoculars with more limited magnification and field of view (center) and roof prism binoculars, generally the most expensive but offering the best optics.

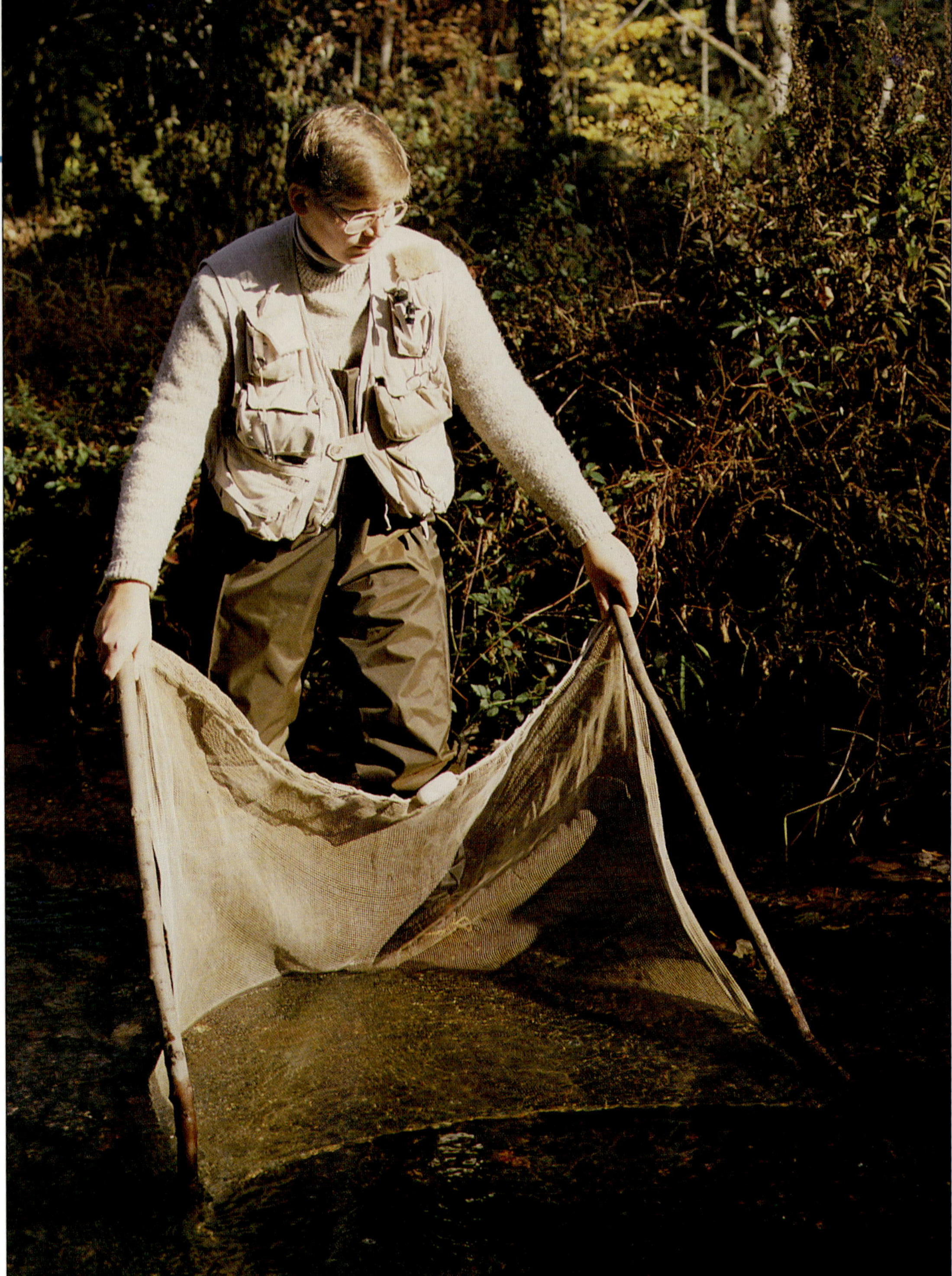

RIGHT A four-foor-square minnow seine is ideal for sampling aquatic life in small streams; it works best if one person holds the net while another wades downstream, chasing minnows and stirring up invertebrates.

NETS

For studying aquatic life, nets are essential. There are two types – dip nets and seines.

Dip nets are built along the same lines as an insect collector's butterfly net, but made of sturdier mesh and with a shallower bag; they can be purchased from science supply centers, or more cheaply made by hand from fine nylon mesh, a wire rim and four- or six-foot wooden handle. Dip nets are good for capturing small, free-swimming insect larvae, fish and amphibians.

For sampling larger areas, you'll need a seine – a long, heavy net designed for catching fish. Most commercially made seines have quarter-inch mesh, lead weights on the bottom edge and foam floats on the top, and cords at each corner to attach poles. The sizes vary from four feet square (ideal for streams) to seines more than 100 feet long and four feet deep, used for sampling lakes, ponds and estuaries. As is emphasized in the section on sampling aquatic life, some states regulate the use of seines, so check local laws before buying or using one.

Although not technically a net, another handy tool for underwater sampling is a metal kitchen strainer with a wooden handle; the eight-inch diameter size is a good choice. Because the strainers are more rugged than cloth nets, they can better stand punishing uses, like scooping up bottom gravel to capture burrowing mayflies.

BLINDS

Blinds – "hides" in Europe – are the most effective way to observe wildlife at close range, without disturbing it, but they present several important drawbacks. Blinds are expensive to buy, time-consuming to build, cumbersome to carry, and severely restrict your mobility. Worst of all, if improperly used they can cause severe disruption to an animal's life.

Blinds can be as elaborate or simple as you desire. The most common model has a collapsible metal pole framework, covered with canvas or nylon; viewing ports are cut in the front and sides, and a zippered door in the back. Setting up such a blind is major operation, and the activity may cause a nesting bird or denning mammal to flee the area. Some naturalists erect large blinds over a period of several days, allowing the animal to become used to it in stages. Others argue that it is better to set the blind up quickly so the disturbance is over with in short order. Regardless, do not erect a blind without serious thought beforehand to its effects on the wildlife you want to watch.

When entering a blind, use the old "two-in, one-out" trick. Have a friend walk to the blind with you, enter, then leave the area. Many birds and other animals, unable to count, will believe that danger is gone, and will return.

A less intrusive (and much cheaper) alternative is a portable "blind" of camouflage clothing. Dressed in camouflage, with a headnet or grease paint and gloves to hide the face and hands, creep into position and sit quietly. Hunters and photographers have long known that personal camouflage causes less disturbance than building a blind, especially with wary animals, but the key is immobility, since most creatures are sensitive to motion. A large piece of camouflage netting, draped over dead branches, will work as a mini-blind to conceal small movements, if you must take notes or use a camera. Where possible, position yourself downwind from mammals (birds have little or no sense of smell, so will be unconcerned by human scent).

Surprisingly, one of the best kinds of blinds may be one you already own – an automobile. A car hides you from view, and is something familiar – and therefore safe – to the animal. Come to a stop slowly and avoid backing up (the change in direction often frightens wildlife). Stay inside, and if you can, keep the windows up. Cars make exceptionally good photo blinds, and there are even special camera and spotting scope mounts that clamp to the window.

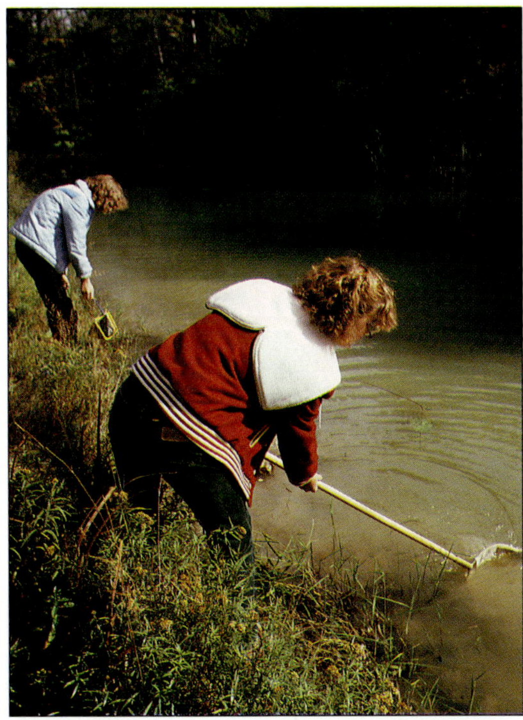

LEFT Dip nets can be cheaply assembled from old broom handles, heavy wire rims and sturdy nylon mesh.

KEEPING A FIELD NOTEBOOK AND JOURNAL

Memory is fallible tool, which is why it is so important to keep accurate notes on what you see in the outdoors, if only for your own use. In the depth of winter it is refreshing to turn to a journal entry from early spring, complete with descriptions of blooming wildflowers and balmy days.

The field notebook has always been more a fixture of British naturalists, especially birders, than it has in North America. There, when a bird-watcher comes across an unfamiliar species, its field marks are carefully noted, usually with a small sketch pointing out the important features; it is only later, at home, that a field guide is consulted and an identification made. This kind of approach, which places an emphasis on careful observation, has a great deal to recommend it, and not just for birds. Recording what you see forces you to look more closely, almost always with salutary effects.

You can use anything as a field notebook, including torn sheets of tablet paper, but it is obviously better to keep your notes in a compact, weatherproof holder. Many naturalists use small, wire-bound artist's sketchbooks, while others prefer looseleaf notebooks that can be replenished periodically, and the notes transferred at the end of a trip to a permanent record at home. Many nature supply companies now offer special zippered field notebook holders of waterproof fabric, many with a shoulder strap and pockets for writing utensils, hand lenses and the like.

What you use is not nearly as important as the fact that you carry it afield and use it. And don't let a lack of writing or artistic

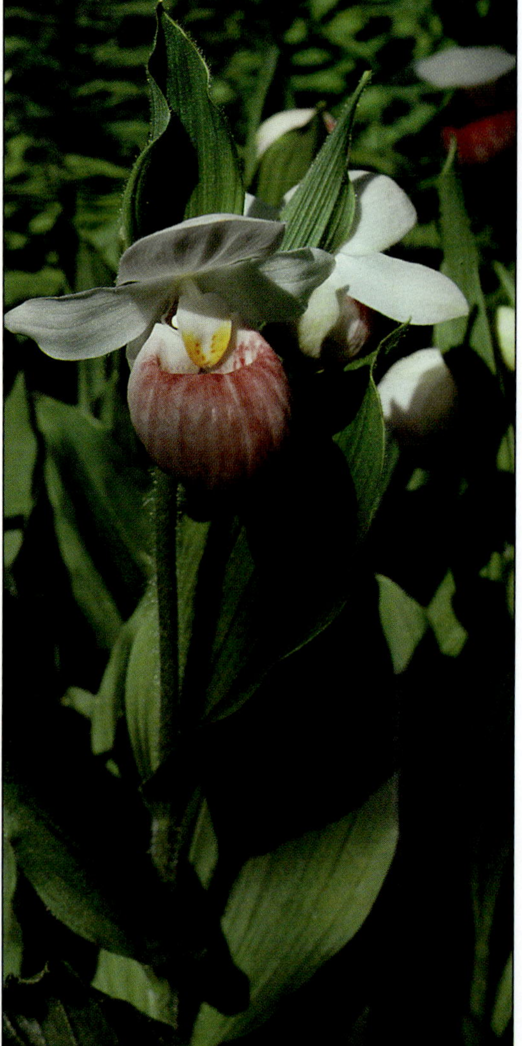

RIGHT Memories fade, but by keeping track of your outdoor observations in a journal or field notebook, you can come to predict what to expect when – for instance, when to expect the showy lady's slippers to bloom.

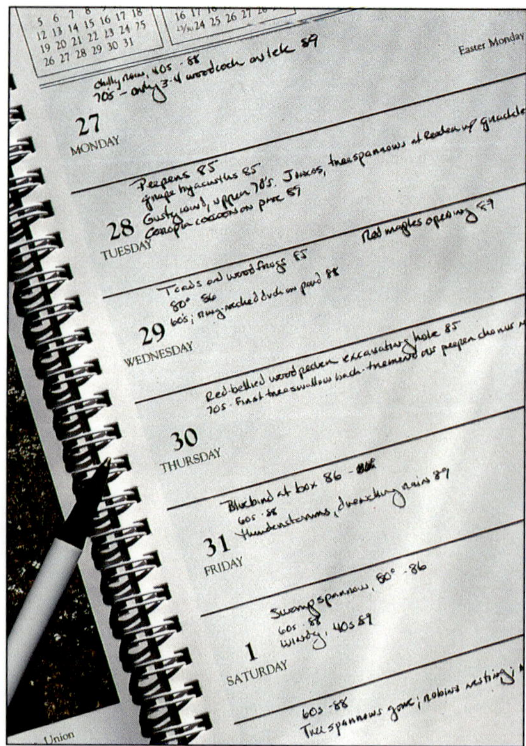

FAR RIGHT A "perpetual notebook" is nothing more than a desk calendar, used year after year for brief notes on outdoor occurrences.

OPPOSITE PAGE A field notebook can be as simple or fancy as you wish. The author's includes small watercolor sketches, along with checklists and journal entries.

talent stop you; the notes are for your benefit alone, not for exhibit, so do not worry if your sketch of a kestrel's head pattern is a little lopsided.

A journal is an extension of the field notebook – a diary of natural events, so to speak. Like the field notebook, it can be as simple or elaborate as you wish. At its heart, a field journal is a daily log of your observations, both great and small – the first day that the hepatica blooms, a checklist from a birding trip, a description of an especially beautiful sunset. By keeping a journal, you create a record of nature's rhythms and happenings in your neighborhood – a record that you will find to be of increasing value as the years go on. When should you expect the thrushes to return in the spring? Check your journal for arrival dates in years gone by. When will the yellow lady's slippers bloom in the bog? The journal will have the answer – an accumulation of all your past outdoor experiences at your fingertips.

Perhaps the simplest form of field journal is a revolving calendar. Buy one of those weekly desk calendars that have space to log engagements for each day – but instead of jotting down dentist appointments, briefly record what you see, with a notation of the year:

> MARCH 17 –
> Woodcock males courting in orchard 1990.
>
> Migrating ring-billed gulls, tundra swans 1991.
>
> Large flocks of geese going north 1992.

Keep using the same calendar year after year (the days of the week won't match up after the first year). Chances are the daily spaces for spring and summer will fill up first; when they finally do, transfer the information to a large, looseleaf notebook, and start with a fresh calendar.

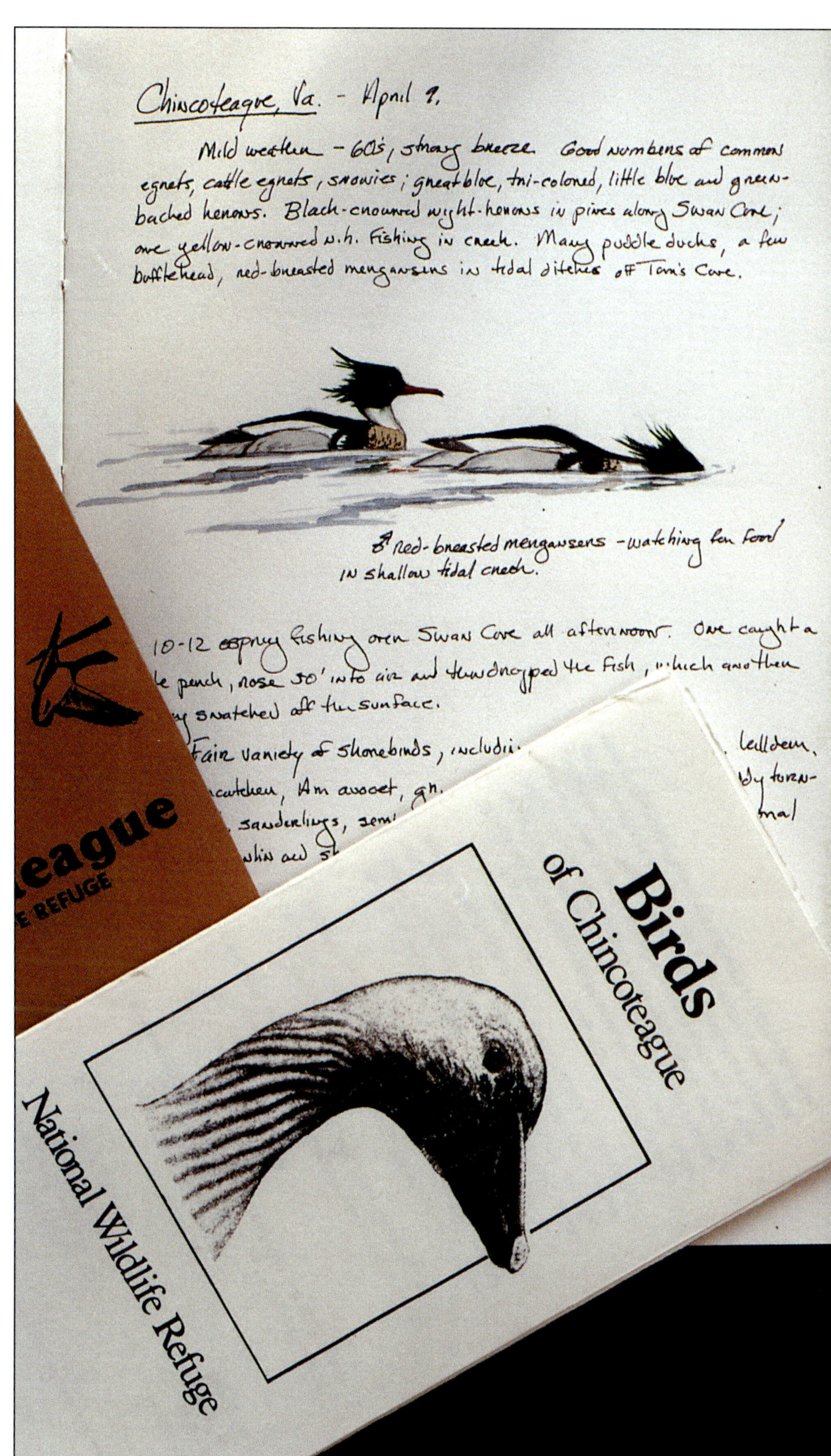

CHAPTER THREE

Activities

RAISING BUTTERFLY AND MOTH CATERPILLARS

RECOMMENDED EQUIPMENT

- Rearing containers
- Constant supply of fresh food plants
- Field guides to butterflies and moths

NOTHING IN NATURE is as magical as the transformation from worm-like caterpillar to graceful butterfly or moth – and few activities are as satisfying as raising several of these beautiful insects through their many stages of development.

While butterfly and moth eggs or larvae can be purchased from commercial breeders, it is often more fun to find them in the wild. To be successful, this requires some research beforehand. Each species has its own preferred food plants – sometimes a single variety of plant, sometimes a wide-ranging group. Finding out what moths and butterflies are common in your area, and their tastes in food plants, will greatly increase your chances of success.

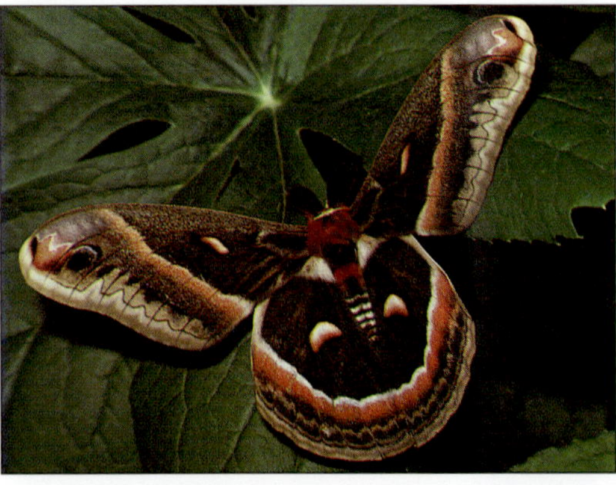

RIGHT The spectacular cecropia moth is the largest of the common silkworm moths, and its baggy cocoon is often found clinging to shrubs and low vines.

The eggs will be small and hard, laid singly or in tight-packed clusters. Do not try to remove the individual eggs (which will kill them), but rather take the entire plant, or a piece if it is too large. More often you'll find the caterpillars, since they are more visible than the tiny eggs. Butterfly and moth larvae go through several growth stages, called instars, and their appearance can change drastically from instar to instar; some field guides illustrate the more common caterpillars.

Avoid handling them any more than necessary, especially in the smallest instars, when careless pressure can injure them. Caterpillars require little specialized care, but their few demands must be met. The first concern is a proper rearing container, which must combine fresh food and a proper place to pupate. Some butterfly enthusiasts use plastic shoe boxes, with screen tops, while others make tall, cylindrical tubes of window screening. Perhaps the easiest model incorporates a large clay flowerpot as the base, with a branch (anchored in pebbles) rising from the middle. Fine netting is simply draped over the branch and cinched to the pot with a rubber band.

Even if the species you are raising eats a wide range of food, supply it with the plant on which it was originally found. Replace the food when it wilts badly, and be sure to collect from areas that have not been sprayed with pesticides or herbicides.

When the caterpillar reaches its final instar, it will prepare to pupate (always be sure the larvae have enough food, because malnutrition will force them to pupate too early, with disastrous results). The caterpillar may seem restless, moving incessantly around its container. How and where it pupates will depend on the species, and the right conditions must be supplied – dead leaves, a branch from which to hang, or a rough vertical surface to attach a silk pad to. Check several field guides or books on the natural history of butterflies and moths, for once again, research beforehand is the key to avoiding problems.

The chrysalis or cocoon is fragile, and should not be disturbed unless absolutely necessary. The pupation period will most likely be several weeks, and it is usually a good idea to spray the casing with a fine mist of water every few days, unless the climate is humid. The emergence of the adult is a time fraught with dangers. The wings are, at first, limp and tightly curled, and are easily damaged by the lightest bump. The adult pumps fluid from its greatly distended abdomen through veins into the wings, unfurling and stretching them; the wings dry and harden as the fluid dissipates. During emergence, the moth or butterfly must have enough room to completely open its wings, or they will dry crumpled and useless.

The adult can be released immediately, or kept for captive breeding. Adult butterflies will need a constant source of nectar or sugar water, while some moths do not feed in their adult stage, surviving only long enough to breed.

Butterflies court visually, usually mating soon after emergence, but female moths attract mates through powerful sexual odors that the males detect with their large, bushy antennae. A female silk moth, kept outside in a netting cage or lightly tethered with soft thread tied gently around the thorax (the middle section of the body), will quickly attract males, which can be allowed to mate with the female.

Butterflies and moths may overwinter as larvae (such as wooly bear caterpillars), pupae (the silk moths) or adults (like the mourning cloak butterfly). If you decide to overwinter captive specimens, keep them refrigerated (not frozen) until spring. Even a short stay in the refrigerator, followed by a return to room temperature, will cause pupae to emerge, so don't take them out prematurely.

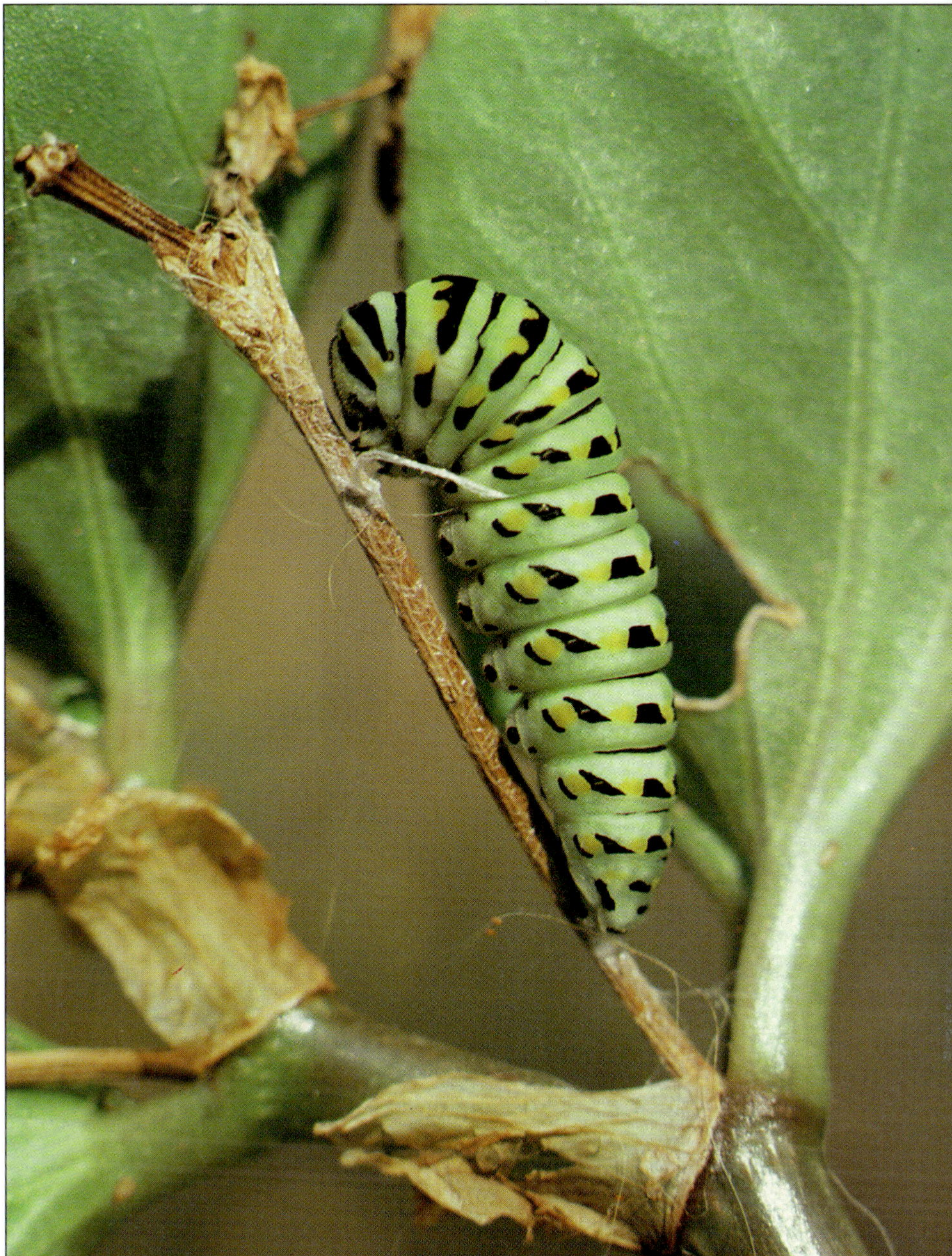

ABOVE A black swallowtail caterpillar prepares to pupate, first spinning two straps of silk to hold itself upright; later it will molt into the pupal stage, changing from a green caterpillar to a brown, mummy-like chrysalid.

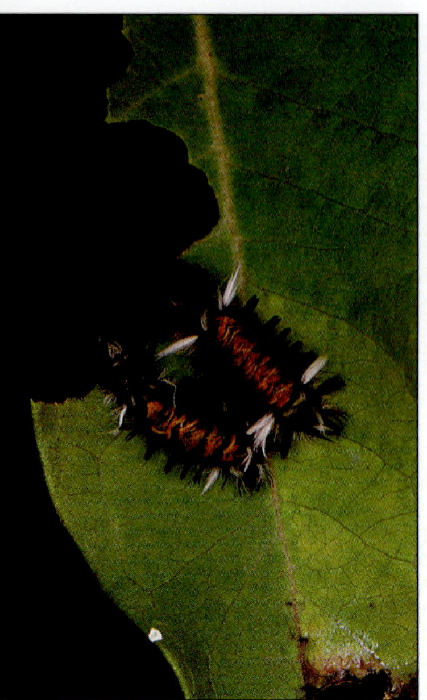

ABOVE Larval food is just as important for butterflies and moths as is nectar for the adults. These milkweed tussock moth caterpillars are feeding on the leaves of the common milkweed, an important food plant for several species.

PLANTING A BUTTERFLY AND HUMMINGBIRD GARDEN

Even the loveliest garden is improved by butterflies drifting on the wind from blossom to blossom, or the frenetic energy of hummingbirds glowing in the sun. Almost any collection of flowers will attract a few butterflies and hummingbirds, but by catering to their tastes and preferences instead of counting on luck, you can make your yard a magnet for them.

Hummingbirds and adult butterflies are both seeking nectar, but they do so in different ways. Hummingbirds have long bills and even longer tongues, and will lap the nectar inside the flower while hovering in front of the blossom; for this reason, they prefer tubular flowers that droop, or are borne away from potentially interfering foliage. Butterflies, on the other hand, alight before drinking, so the flowers they patronize are usually wide and flat, with many small florets into which the butterfly pokes its uncurled proboscis.

For butterflies, the best – and easiest – nectar-bearing flowers are members of the enormous composite family, which includes such favorites as zinnias, marigolds, ox-eye daisies (*Chrysanthemum leucanthemum*) and asters. Composites, with their disk florets, rely on insect pollination, and so provide ample nectar as a bribe for butterflies, honeybees, hover flies and other pollinators. Many of the wild or "old fashioned" varieties retain colors and patterns that direct flying insects to the nectar – especially when viewed under ultraviolet light, which is how many insects see the world.

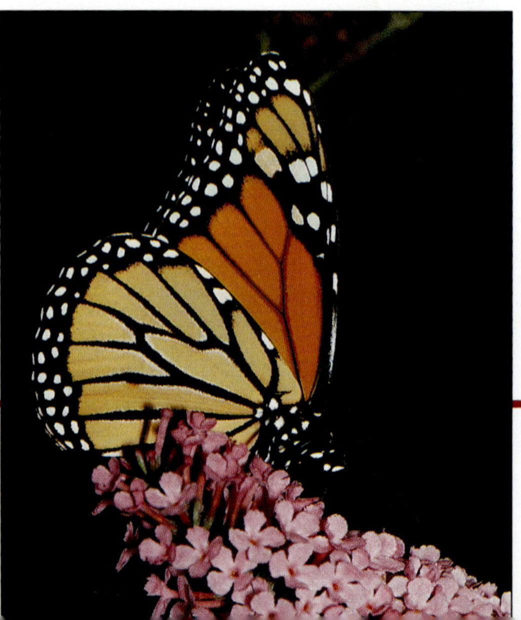

RIGHT The aptly-named butterfly bush *(Buddleia)* attracts an adult monarch, one of the most common visitors to a well-planted garden.

Not all good butterfly plants are spectacular, and some "weeds" are outstanding for their attraction value. The milkweed family is an excellent case in point; common milkweed (*Asclepias syriaca*) and its smaller cousin swamp milkweed (*A. incarnata*), which also grows in damp fields, are terrific for attracting late-summer butterflies. So are the many varieties of native goldenrod, which – contrary to public perception – are not a hay fever hazard, since their pollen is not wind-borne. Queen Anne's lace (*Daucus carota*), a member of the wild carrot family, is another good butterfly attractant usually overlooked because it is so common.

The choice of hummingbird plants is only slightly smaller. Impatiens, garden sage (*Salvia*) and flowering tobacco (*Nicotiana*) top the list of annuals, while beebalm (*Monarda*), coral bells (*Heuchara*) and scarlet penstemon (*Penstemon*) are excellent perennials. Good shrubs include trumpet creeper (*Campsis radicans*) – perhaps the best of all hummingbird plants – and buttonbush (*Cephalanthus*), while flowering quince (*Chaenomeles*) is superb for early spring, just when the hummers return from their wintering grounds.

The hummingbird's fondness for red is well known, and probably somewhat over-stated. While some hummingbirds, like the ruby-throat of the East, do seem to be attracted to red, they diligently investigate flowers of almost any hue. The quantity of nectar, rather than the color, keeps them coming back for more.

When choosing domestic flowers for either butterflies or hummingbirds, select single forms, rather than those that bear double blossoms, which may be too thick for the bird or insect to penetrate. Similarly, older varieties of popular garden plants usually produce more nectar than newer hybrids, and so are a better choice.

In addition to nectar-producing plants, it is possible to increase the number of

SUGGESTED PLANTS FOR BUTTERFLIES

Butterfly weed (*Asclepias tuberosa*)
•
Zinnias
•
Asters (Genus *Aster*)
•
Marigolds
•
Coreopsis
•
Native goldenrods
•
Lavender or hyssop
•
Butterfly bush (*Buddleia*)
•
Mock-orange
•
Lilac
•
Clover or alfalfa, parsley, milkweed (food plants)

SUGGESTED PLANTS FOR HUMMINGBIRDS

Garden sage (*Salvia*)
•
Bee-balm (*Monarda*)
•
Buttonbush (*Cephalanthus*)
•
Trumpet creeper (*Campsis radicans*)
•
Impatiens
•
Flowering tobacco (*Nicotiana*)
•
Flowering quince
•
Butterfly bush (*Buddleia*)

butterflies around your garden by planting food for their caterpillars. Each species has a specific group of plants, or even a single plant, on which its larvae can feed – milkweed for the monarch and Queen butterflies, members of the carrot family (including Queen Anne's lace and parsley) for black swallowtails, sheep sorrel for American coppers, and alfalfa or white clover for sulphurs.

Many butterflies are also attracted to mud puddles, especially those around farmyards where the liquid is laced with urine or manure. You can replicate this more pleasantly in the garden by lining a small depression in the soil with plastic, then filling it with sand; water well with the hose each day to keep it damp. A half-bottle of beer or fruit juice serves as a further incentive.

Obviously, when gardening for butterflies and hummingbirds, stop using pesticides entirely; most garden sprays are non-specific, and will kill insects indiscriminately, as well as being dangerous to hummingbirds drinking tainted nectar. Furthermore, many chemicals linger for weeks or months before breaking down into less harmful compounds, and while they last that can be tranferred through the food chain, eventually damaging wildlife the gardener never intended to harm.

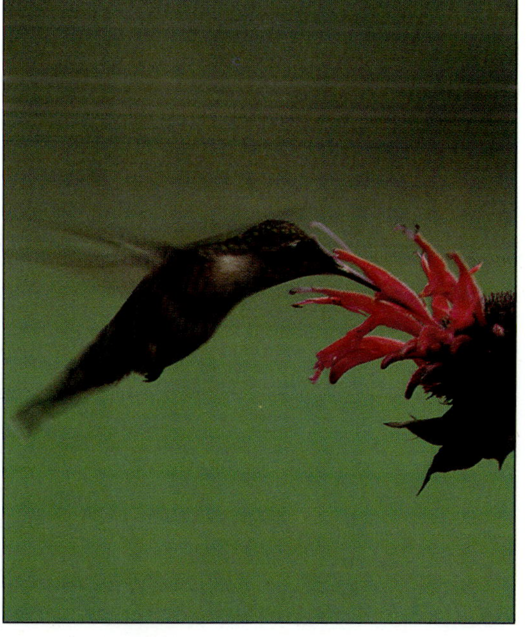

LEFT A female ruby-throated hummingbird hovers at a bee-balm *(Monarda)* flower, which with its tubular blossoms is perfectly suited to a hummingbird's long, probing bill.

EXPLORING THE LIFE OF A ROTTEN LOG

RECOMMENDED EQUIPMENT
- Hand lens

It is a basic principle in the science of ecology that life proceeds from death, and nowhere is that more obvious than on a fallen, rotting log. What was once a living tree provides food and housing for a multitude of plants and animals, from microscopic organisms to bears.

A large, rotting log is an ecosystem in itself, as distinct from the forest around it as a marsh is distinct from a meadow. For your exploration, choose a log that is somewhere in its middle ages of decomposition – not too fresh and hard, still resisting the attacks of roots and jaws, but not too far gone into the process, a long hump of crumbling humus.

All you need is a hand lens and patience. Examine the outside of the log first. There will probably be fungi of some form growing on it – perhaps multicolored shelf fungi in clamshell-shaped conks, or stemmed mushrooms. Fungi lack chlorophyll, the chemical that green plants use to create food through the process of photosynthesis. For this reason, they must rely on plants or animals for their food, just as animals rely, ultimately, on green plants for their sustenance. Saprophytic fungi, like those that grow on rotting logs, live on dead organic matter – in this case, the dead cellulose of the tree. Some are also parasitic, infecting live trees through injured areas, and can eventually kill their host.

Sharing the outer rim of the log with the fungi may be lichens and mosses, especially if the log is lying in a moist area. Lichens are actually a juncture of two distinct living things – fungi and algae, a saprophyte and a green plant, so closely joined together that they function as (and

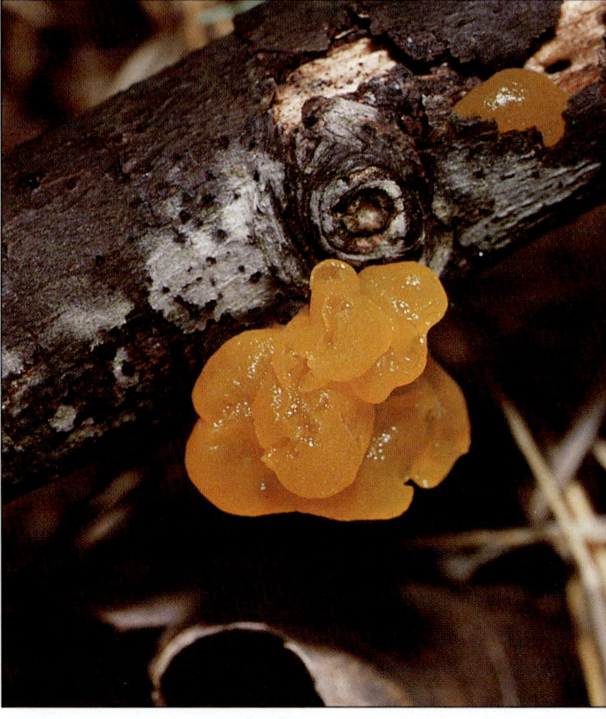

can therefore be considered to be) a single organism. The fungal half of the equation supplies the lichen with water and nutrients from the log, while the algal component, with its chlorophyll, can photosynthesize the nutrients and water into food.

Moss is a true green plant, and one of the oldest plant groups on Earth, but its life history is radically different from flowering plants that evolved later. Mosses reproduce through spores, which grow into something very similar to a simple alga. What we think of as the moss itself is really a fuzzy, sexual stalk that grows off this alga-like stage; the sexual stage, in turn, supports a parasitic stage that produces spores for the next generation.

The rotting log is also rich habitat for insects and other arthropods. Flake off a section of bark, or peel away a piece of the outer layer of wood. Just under the bark, you may find the borings of engraver beetles, which cut a delicate – and for the live tree, dangerous – tracery of tunnels. Although the engraver beetles do not live in rotting logs, many other species of beetle do, along with ants, spiders, isopods (also known as wood lice or pillbugs), centipedes and millipedes. Look very closely, and you may see tiny flecks of brilliant red moving across the wood. These are velvet mites, harmless, spider-like arthropods that feed on insect eggs.

Not all of the rotting log's life is minute. Grubs and insects attract black bears, which may spend the better part of a day ripping a large log into chunks and feeding on its inhabitants. Hollow logs provide denning sites for raccoons, opossums, foxes and other mammals (look for tracks, scat or hair), and overhead protection for ground-nesting birds like ruffed grouse, ovenbirds and wild turkeys. Biologists have found that the number of mice, voles and shrews in a forest is directly tied to the abundance of fallen logs, which provide pathways, den sites and escape routes for small mammals – and which, in turn, attract larger predators. A fallen log may look unimportant or even wasteful, but it goes on "living," in terms of food and shelter for other organisms, for many, many years.

ABOVE LEFT Gelatinous slime molds erupt from a decomposing branch – one of many saprophytic organisms that draw their life from the dead wood.

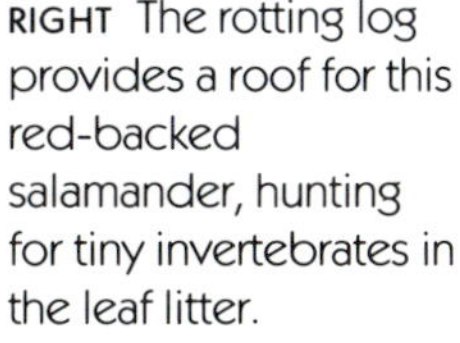

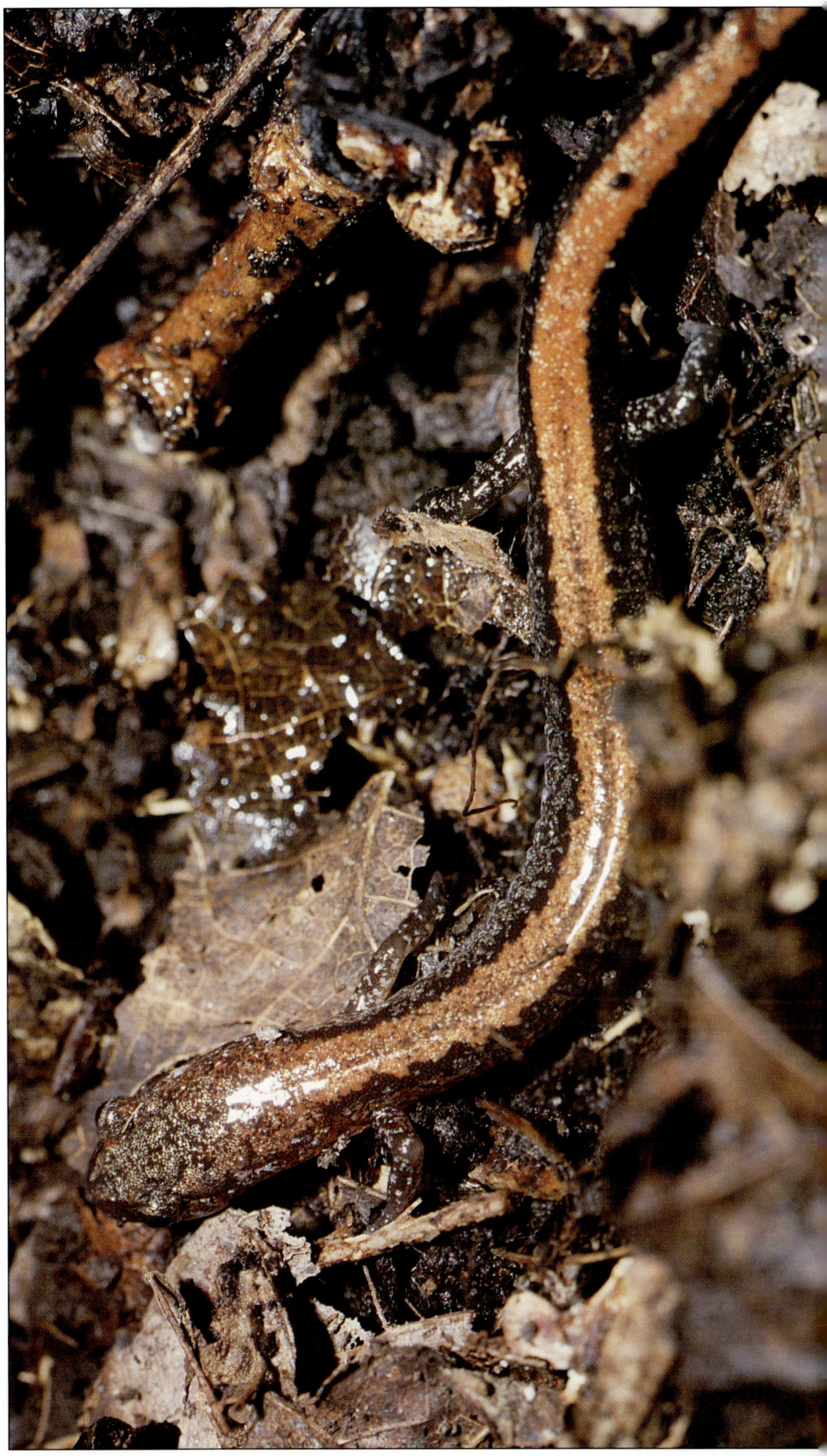

RIGHT The rotting log provides a roof for this red-backed salamander, hunting for tiny invertebrates in the leaf litter.

TRACKING DOWN A WILD BEE TREE

RECOMMENDED EQUIPMENT

- Small dish of sugar water (two parts sugar to five parts water)
- Oil of peppermint (optional)
- Fine artist's paintbrush
- Blue carpenter's chalk
- Compass (optional)

There is some argument over the origin of honeybees in North America. While some authorities consider them a native part of the continent's wildlife, others believe that the bees were brought to these shores by the first European colonists.

Although most honeybee hives are in domestic apiaries, there are wild colonies in almost areas – a fact that country people exploited when they had the urge for something sweet-tasting. The hard part is finding the wild hive, usually secreted in a hollow tree. It takes a lot of luck to stumble onto a hive, but there is an easier way.

Bees travel fairly long distances for nectar, and once having found a good supply, return to the hive and do a unique, body-waggling dance, oriented to the sun's position, that tells the other bees in the hive in what direction and at what distance the food may be found. Traveling from the food to the hive, the bees will take a direct course – a "beeline" in the truest sense.

To track down a bee colony, fill a shallow bowl with a concentrated sugar water mix and place it on a stump, or on the ground. Some of the frontier bee hunters burned a small quantity of beeswax, which was said to attract them as well, and a few drops of oil of peppermint in the sugar water will help draw bees. While you're waiting for the bees to find you – which shouldn't take too long, especially on a warm day – grind some blue carpenter's chalk to produce a fine powder.

When the honeybees are feeding eagerly on the sugar water, pick up a dab of chalk on a fine-tipped paintbrush and mark the back of one or two of the bees; do it gently, and the mild-tempered honeybee shouldn't even pause in her drinking. Then watch carefully. When the bee is finished it will take off, circle above the dish several times, and strike out in the direction of its hive. Note the path of travel as closely as possible, using a compass if you like, and move the dish along it – say, 40 or 50 yards.

Set up the dish again and wait. Before too long (depending on the distance to the hive), your marked bee should return. When it finishes filling up once more, note the flight path and move again, although not quite as far this time. Repeat this procedure each time, and you should find the interval between the bee's departure and arrival decreasing steadily as you near the hive. Eventually, you'll reach a point when the bee takes off in the *opposite* direction – an indication that you've overshot the hive. Now scrutinize every large tree along the path, looking for a hole, knot or cavity that bees are using; a pair of binoculars is invaluable for this.

In the old days, the colony would be stupefied with smoke, the tree cut and the honeycombs taken, while the swarm would be captured and moved to an apiary. From a naturalist's perspective, it is reward enough to have tracked a bee through the air, and discovered its hidden lair, without disturbing it further.

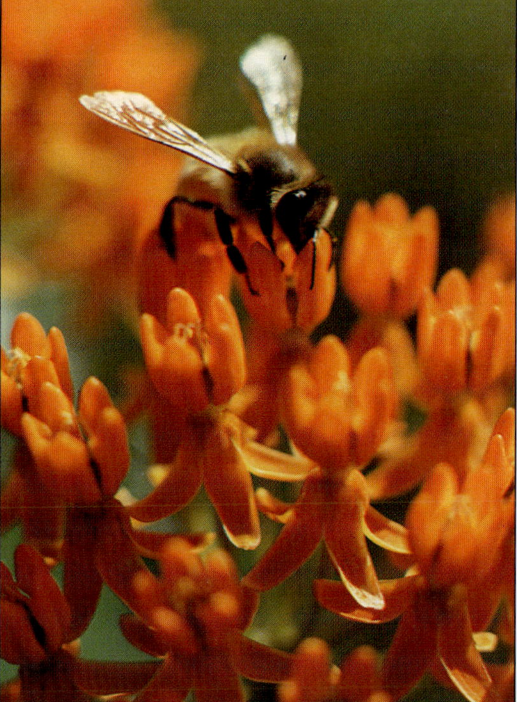

RIGHT By using an ancient technique, it is possible to find the hives of wild honeybees.

"SUGARING" FOR RARELY SEEN MOTHS

RECOMMENDED EQUIPMENT

- Plastic bucket
- Large paintbrush
- Flashlight
- Field guide to moths
- Fruit mash

Because they are nocturnal, moths are far less appreciated for their beauty than are butterflies. Yet many of the moths eclipse even the gaudiest butterflies for size, color and pattern – if you're lucky enough to find them. Many are rarely seen, even though they may be relatively common.

"Sugaring" for moths is an ideal way to attract some of the most unusual species for observation, photography or restrained collecting. It takes advantage of the moth's sensitive odor-detection capabilities, and their taste for rotten fruit.

Sugaring is a spring-to-late-summer activity. Make the bait several days before hand. In a large pail, mix overripe fruit – bananas, peaches and other soft varieties are best – along with molasses or brown sugar, and a bottle of beer, to form a syrupy mash. Cover tightly to keep out flies, and put it somewhere in the sun to ferment for several days – a rooftop is a good choice, since the sweet smell may attract raccoons or other mammals on the ground.

Start sugaring at dusk. You'll want to lay out a circular route along an easily followed path, preferably one that goes through a number of habitats – not just woods, but also along field edges, swamp margins or orchards. Every 30 or 40 yards, pick a large tree and "paint" a hand-sized swath of its trunk with the fruit mash, then move on.

By the time you're finished painting, it should be fully dark. Follow the trail once again, this time with a carefully shielded flashlight. The mash should have attracted a wide variety of insects, from ants to moths; most common among the latter will be the underwing moths of the genus *Catocala*, which have forewings camouflaged like tree bark, against which they hide by day. At night, though, they expose their hindwings – vivid red, orange or pink in some species, banded with black or white; others are more somber, of deep copper or plain black. The best response from the moths will come on warm, humid nights with the threat of thunderstorms, when the scent carries most powerfully through the woods.

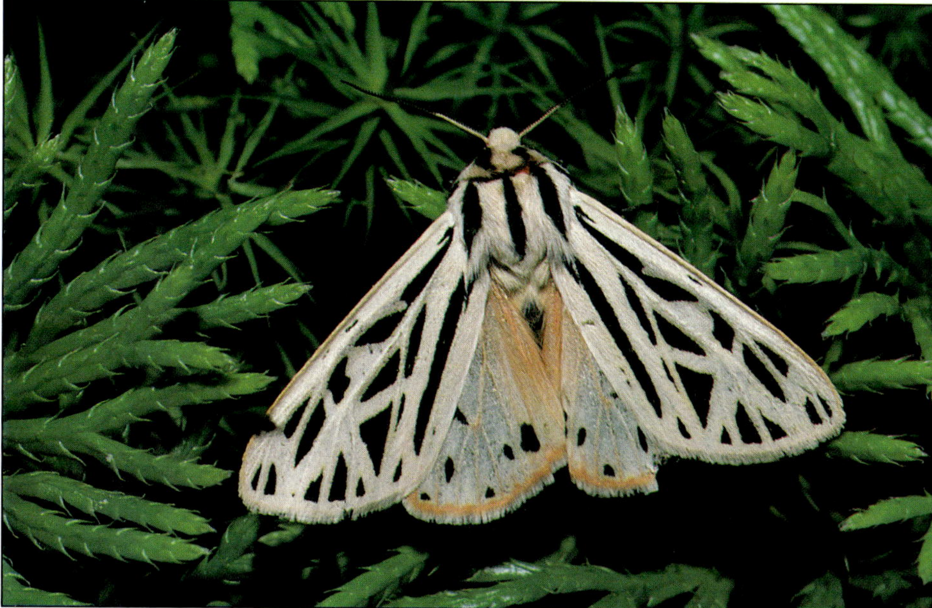

ABOVE Difficult to find despite their brightly patterned wings, the *Apantesis* tiger moths are most easily observed at a sugaring station.

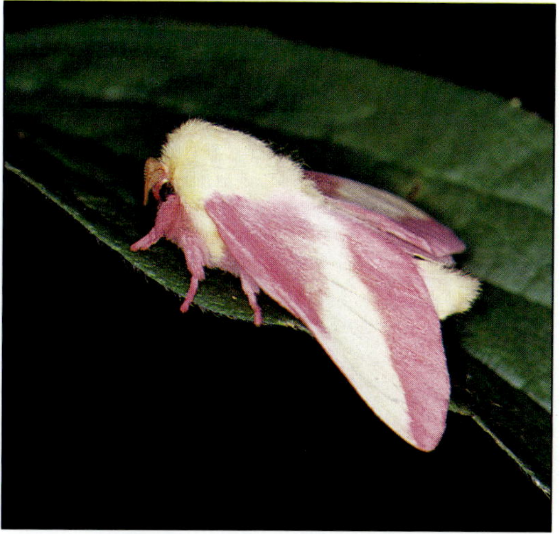

LEFT Pastel shades of pink and yellow make the rosy maple moth one of the most attractive species of night-fliers over much of North America.

RIGHT Barnacles look like shellfish, but they are actually crustaceans that spend their lives cemented to rocks and pilings at the highest reaches of the intertidal zone.

BELOW A pugnacious female rock crab, uncovered from her hiding place in the rockweed, waves her claws to defend her spongy, orange egg mass.

EXPLORING TIDAL POOLS

RECOMMENDED EQUIPMENT

- Hand lens
- White basin or plastic bucket
- Gloves (to prevent barnacle cuts) and tennis shoes

The world between the waves, where land and sea collide in a crash of breakers and the never-ending rise and fall of the tides, is a difficult place for a living thing to make its home. Alternately exposed to dry air and frigid ocean water, a plant or animal must be extraordinarily tough to survive.

On sandy beaches where there is no solid base to withstand the waves, life may seem sparse, although there is much hidden beneath the wet sand. But the best places to observe tidal zone life are along rocky coasts, where the falling tide leaves behind pockets of standing water – the tidal pools. The coast of northern New England and the Canadian Maritimes, and the coast of the Pacific Northwest from northern California to British Columbia, offer the richest chances for discovery.

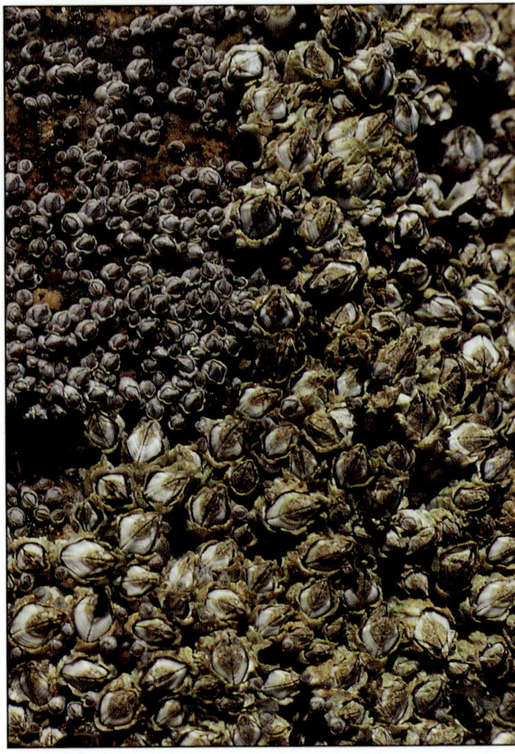

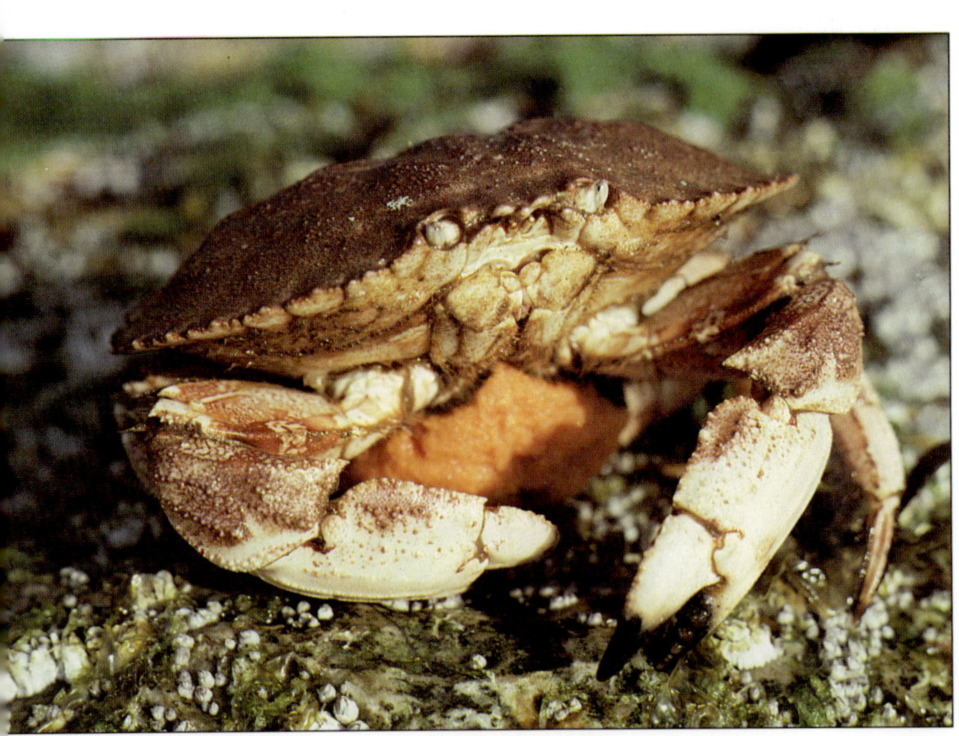

Exactly when you can explore the tidal zone will be controlled by the tide; get a tide chart for the local waters (most tackle shops have them) and try to coincide your visit with low tide. If you can, also try for a visit at full or new moon, when the tides rise highest and drop lowest.

Life in the tidal zone is strictly segregated to certain levels, depending on how much exposure to air each species can tolerate. At a distance, these levels appear as bands of light or dark colors, but up close one can see that they are close-packed plants or animals. The spray zone is the highest, where only the splash of wind-tossed waves wet the rocks. Here, multi-colored lichens grow; a few feet further down, where the spray keeps the rocks moister, can be found blue-green algae growing in dark layers, looking somewhat like paint.

Blue-green alga is one of the most primitive forms of life on Earth, only a step above bacteria, but containing chlorophyll for photosynthesis. The alga is food for periwinkles, snail-like gastropods with shells about 1¼ inches long. Of all the intertidal animals, periwinkles can withstand the longest exposure to sun, simply pulling themselves into their shells to conserve moisture.

In the tidal zone, the difference of a few inches can bring a change in habitat. A foot or two down from the periwinkles is the wide barnacle zone, jammed with their hard, conical shells. Remarkably, barnacles are not mollusks, but crustaceans, relatives of lobsters and crabs. As larvae they are free-swimming creatures, but at an early age they seek out a hard surface (usually a rock) at the correct depth and glue themselves down, head-first, secreting a calcified shell. When the tide rises, the barnacles open the locked top of their shells and use feather-like appendages to kick particles of food into their mouths.

Below the barnacles come layers of blue mussels, each affixed with strong filaments glued fast to the rocks; this zone is only exposed to the air briefly, and at the lowest point of the tide. The mussel beds are the hunting ground of the sea stars, usually (and incorrectly) called starfish, even though they are echinoderms, not fish. Sea stars use their powerful suction feet to pry open a mussel or other shellfish, then invert their stomach into the shell, enveloping the helpless mollusk and digesting it.

In the same tidal pools as the sea stars, look for sea urchins, especially the green sea urchin with its short spines, common on both coasts. By carefully probing beneath mats of rockweed, irish moss and other sea weeds, one can uncover green or rock crabs, hermit crabs hiding in appropriated periwinkle shells, sea anemones, and the odd sea cucumber, a potato-like animal that will expel its entire digestive system if disturbed, then grow a new one at its leisure.

The tidal zone is an exciting place to explore, but it can also be treacherous, with hazards as mild as nipping crabs, or as dangerous as the swirling water. When exploring tidal pools, wear sneakers with good treads, and be exceptionally careful of your footing. Wet rockweed or kelp is treacherous underfoot, and a fall onto sharp barnacles can cause nasty cuts. Most importantly, watch for the returning tide, and don't be cut off from land on an isolated rock shelf. Handle any creatures gently, returning them quickly to the water.

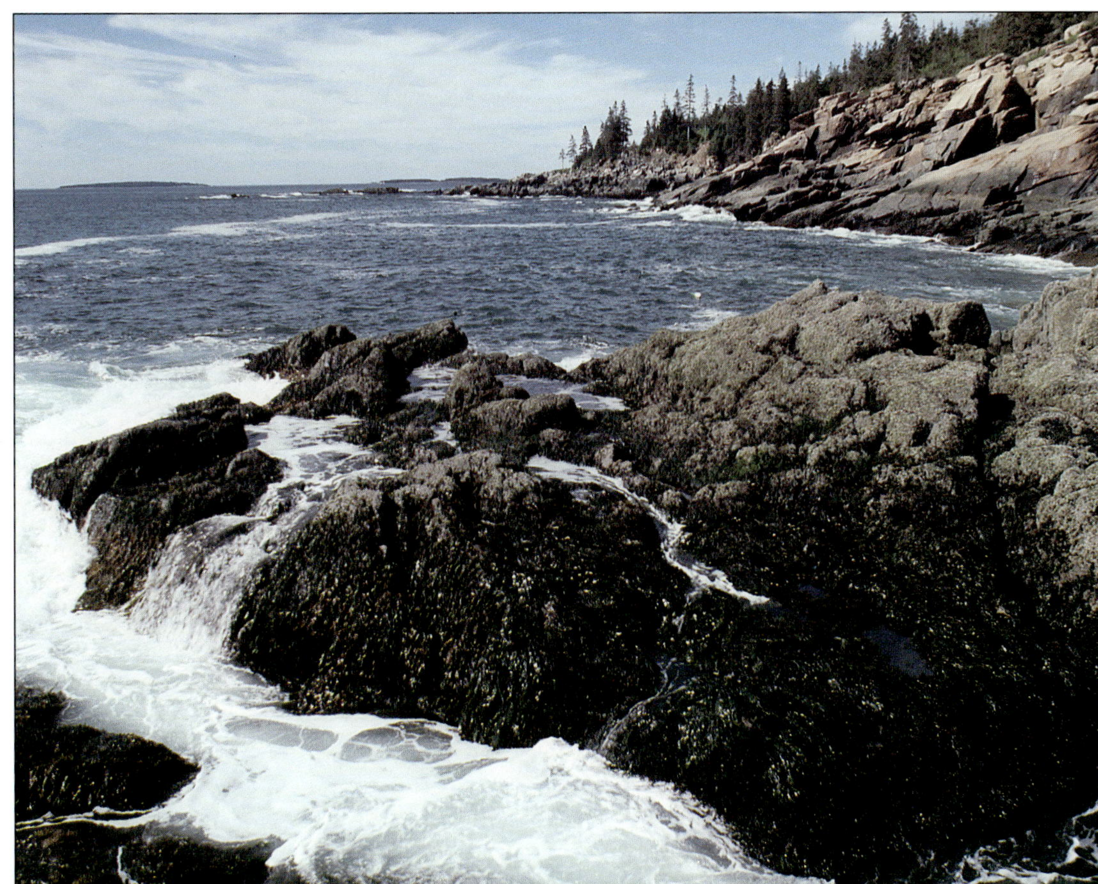

LEFT Areas like the coast of Maine, where the shore is rocky and the difference between high and low tides is great, are the best places for tidal pool study.

SAMPLING AQUATIC LIFE IN STREAMS AND PONDS

RECOMMENDED EQUIPMENT

- 4-by-4-foot seine (streams)
- 4-by-20-foot seine (ponds)
- Dip nets
- Large kitchen strainers
- Hand lens
- White basin
- Hip waders (sneakers and shorts in warm weather)

Within the narrow confines of a stream's banks, and beneath the tranquil surface of a pond, exists an intricately tangled web of life that echoes the larger world around it – a world of predators and prey, of chase and evasion and capture. But the players are lilliputian, and mostly hidden from our view. A seine is the key to unlocking the underwater world. Commonly known as "minnow nets" and available through sporting goods stores, they come in two basic sizes – 4 feet square, or 4-by-20-feet, the latter suited to ponds. (Before using seines, check your state or provincial regulations. Some wildlife agencies restrict the size of seines, while others require a fishing license for their use).

On a stream, a small seine is all that is necessary. Have one person hold the seine where the current is strong, making sure that the weighted bottom edge is flat against the stream bottom. Another person goes upstream a short distance and stirs up sediment to cloud the water, then sloshes slowly downstream to the net, rooting under eroded banks and logs to chase out fish. Quickly remove any captured animals and place them in a basin or bucket for examination. Large metal mesh kitchen strainers are good for sampling small areas.

What you'll find will depend on the stream. Small, cold mountain creeks will

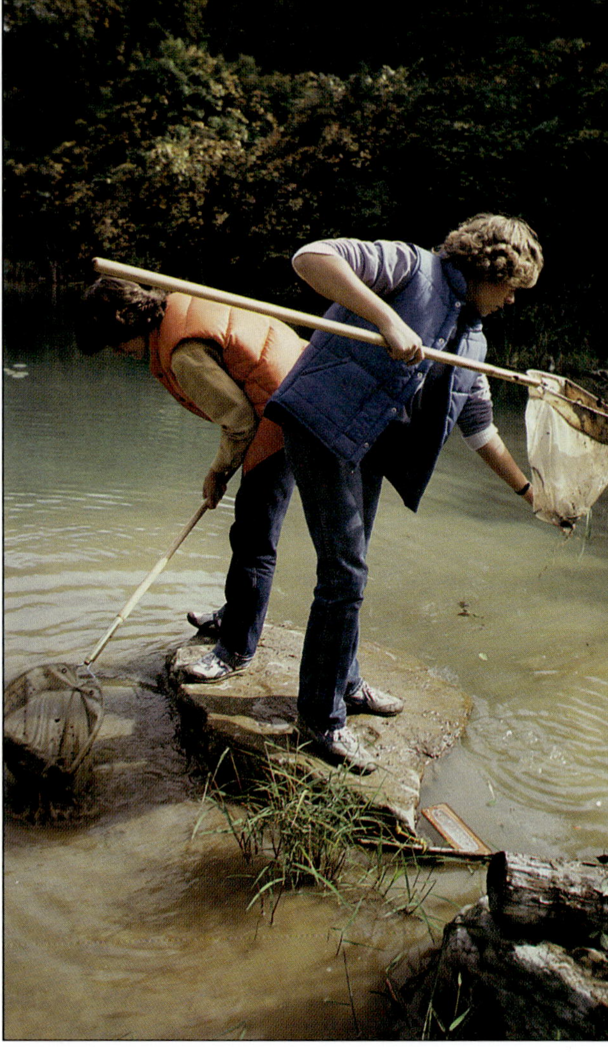

RIGHT Dip nets are effective for capturing small, active animals like tadpoles, minnows and newts.

have insects adapted to life in fast water – mayfly and stonefly larvae that hide beneath rocks, "water pennies" (flattened beetle larvae), and streamlined minnows such as daces or darters. In warmer, slower waters with a silty bottom, expect an abundance of caddisfly larvae, grublike cranefly larvae, crayfish, and warm-water fish like bluegills, bullhead catfish and chubs.

Caddisfly larvae are among the most interesting underwater inhabitants. For the first year of its life, the caddisfly is a soft-bodied, crawling insect. To protect itself, the larva constructs a casing, the materials and shape of which vary from species to species. Some use small twigs, others neatly trimmed sections of leaves,

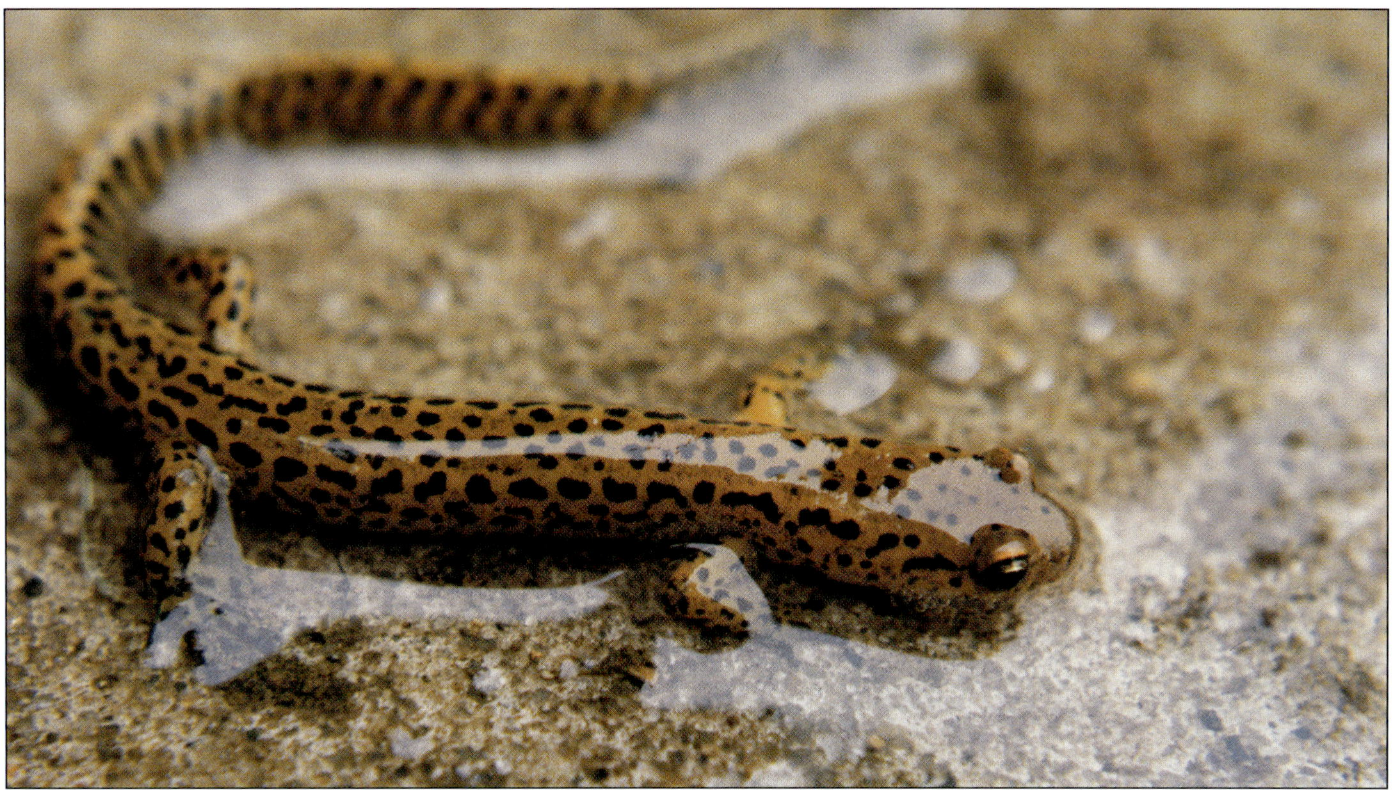

or grains of sand, or living duckweed. Most caddisflies drag their cases along with them, but some remain glued to rocks or logs, and one group even spins a silken web across the current to capture food. The larvae eventually pupate in their cases, and emerge into the air as winged, mothlike adults.

A larger seine is needed to sample ponds. With several people supporting the net and its poles, wade out into a shallow cove, stretch the net and walk slowly to shore, encircling the fish and invertebrates. Dip nets also work well in ponds, especially for capturing frogs, diving beetles and small fish.

In the still water of a pond, it is not necessary to fight the current, so animals are freer to move around. Perhaps the most unusual method of locomotion is that of the dragonfly nymph, which employs a form of jet propulsion. The nymph – dark and flattened, with a bulbous head and prominent jaws – draws water into its body cavity, then forcefully expels it through the rear, pushing itself gracefully through the water. In late spring and summer, look for the empty skin shucks of dragonfly nymphs on branches and emergent vegetation around the pond edge, where the insects climbed out of the water, shed their skin and flew off as the familiar winged adults.

ABOVE A member of the brook salamander group, the long-tailed salamander is found beneath rocks along cold, clear streams.

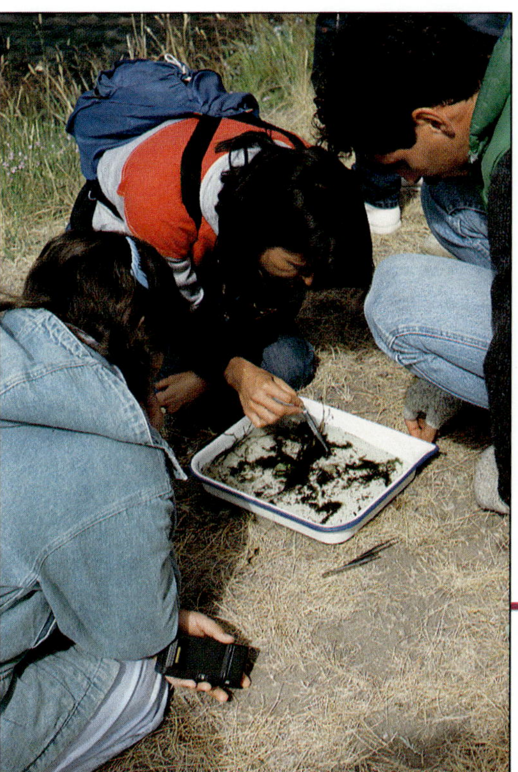

LEFT A white tray is ideal for sorting through leaves and vegetation pulled up in the net; small invertebrates that would otherwise be missed are easy to spot.

MAINTAINING A NATIVE, SHORT-TERM AQUARIUM

After a trip to the local stream or pond, you may want to keep a few of the animals you find for more in-depth study. Maintaining a "native" aquarium is the answer.

Setting up an aquarium takes time, so make all your preparations long before the collecting trip. Essentially the same set-up as is used for tropical fish will work for native species – a tank of at least 10 gallons capacity, a undergravel filter, an air pump and bubble diffusion system (such as air stones) and a light. A heater is not necessary, since in many cases the tank must be kept as cool as possible.

Wash the tank and all the fittings thoroughly with hot, salty water, then rinse completely in plain hot water – use no soap at any time. Washing is especially important if the tank has been used before, since it may harbor diseases or parasites.

Tap water (treated for chlorine if need be) will work fine for native organisms. Do not use pond or creek water, which usually has a great deal of suspended matter in it, and may harbor diseases. Likewise, any rocks or gravel from local waters must be thoroughly washed and subjected to boiling water rinses; it is generally better to use store-bought materials. Set up the tank and get everything running at least a week before adding any fish or invertebrates.

Not every creature you net from a pond or stream is going to survive in an aquarium. Organisms from cold, fast-flowing streams are extremely difficult to maintain in the aquarium, requiring power filters, high oxygenation and a refrigeration system to keep the water temperature under 48°F. A better idea is to collect from a warm pond,

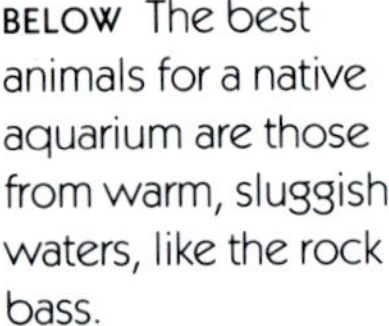

BELOW The best animals for a native aquarium are those from warm, sluggish waters, like the rock bass.

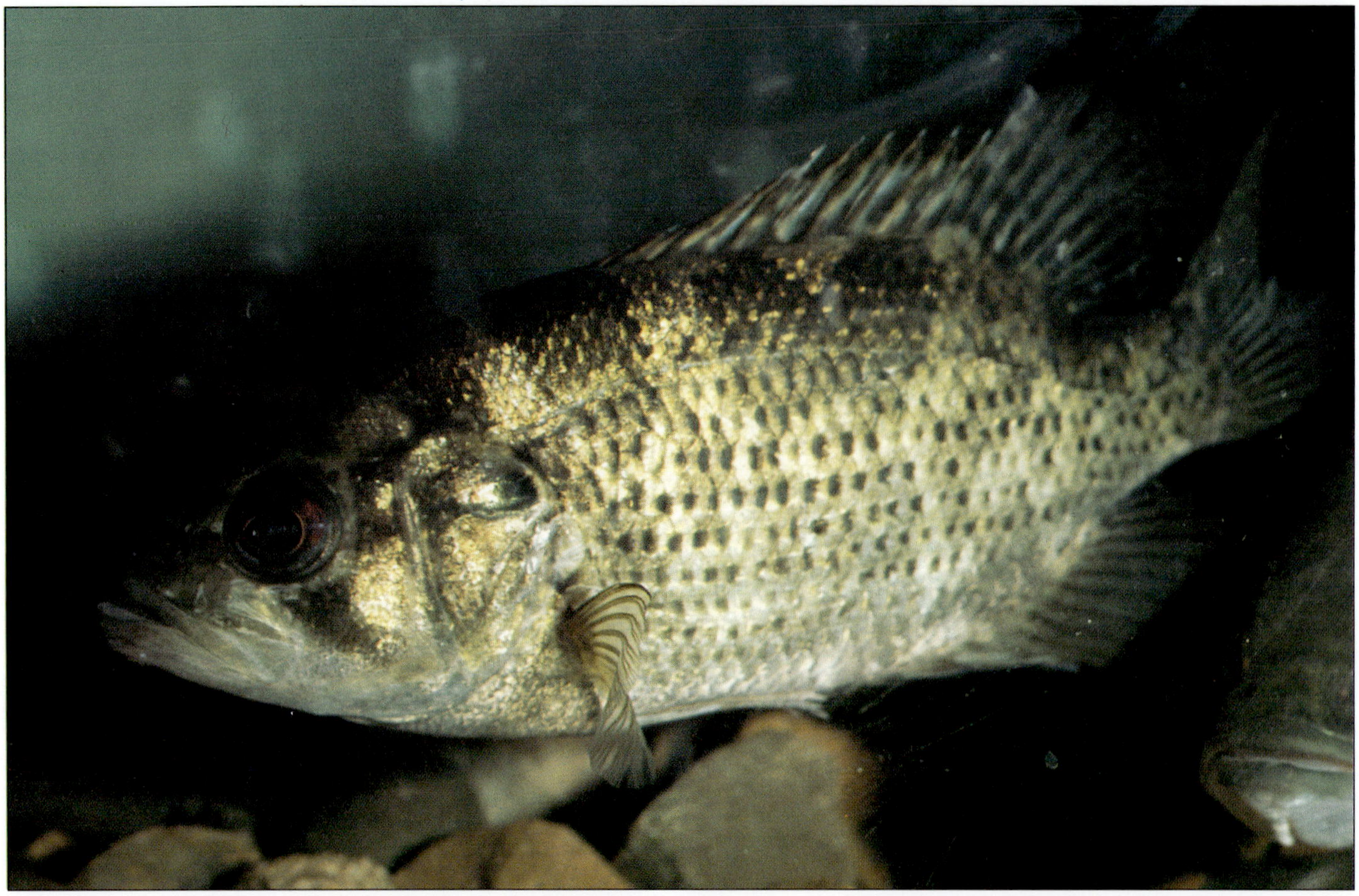

which contains animals pre-adapted to conditions in a tank. Minnows, sunfish and small bullheads all do well in captivity, as do perch, shiners and mosquito fish. As with sampling, be sure to check local conservation regulations, which may restrict what species (and under what circumstances) can be taken.

To transport your catch, use large, doubled plastic bags, half-filled with water (the trapped air will oxygenate the water). At home, put the fish into a large, clean bucket, with an airstone and a few inches of water. Then run a siphon – air tubing will do – from the tank to the bucket, and crimp the tubing with a clothespin so the siphon trickles slowly. As the bucket fills, the fish will be gently acclimated to the temperature and mineral composition of the tank water.

Invertebrates also make good candidates for the native aquarium – in fact, an all-invertebrate tank can be fascinating. Small crayfish, freshwater clams and mussels, and a host of insect larvae are all good choices. Some, while interesting, will wreak havoc; predators like dragonfly larvae will systematically pick off smaller invertebrates, fish and tadpoles. The same goes for predaceous diving beetles and their larvae "water tigers" and the elegantly sinister water scorpion, an elongated bug that breathes through two slender tubes projecting from its rear.

Of course, everything has to eat, and you may want to watch such predator/prey dramas in your tank. The proper food is obviously important for all tank-dwellers. Wild-caught fish will probably spurn prepared fish food, especially flake varieties, but should accept frozen brine shrimp or finely diced raw fish. Feed only as much as

BELOW Small turtles (this is a juvenile red-eared turtle) can be kept in the native aquarium, but must have a place to crawl completely from the water to bask.

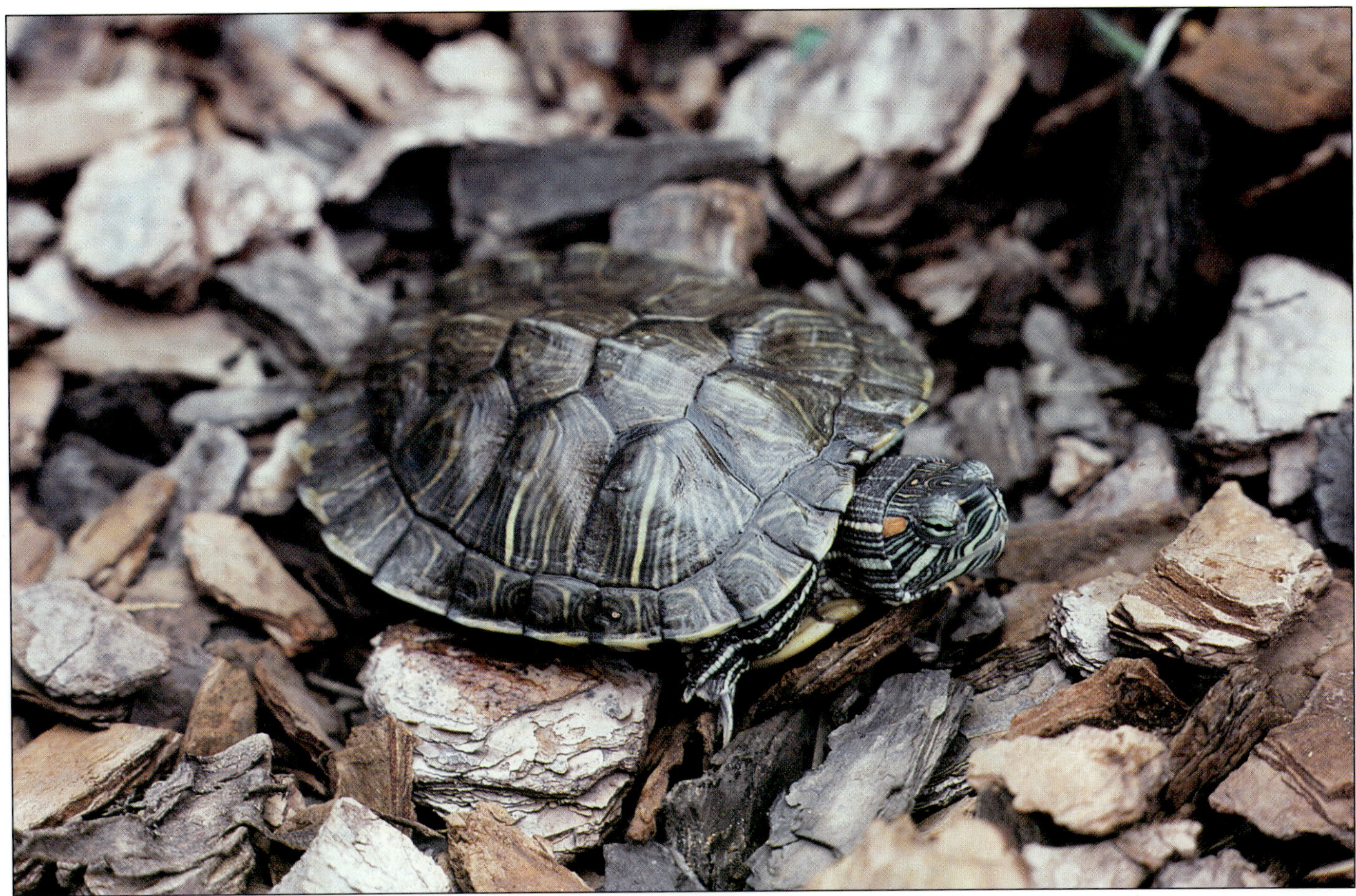

the fish will eat in a few minutes; any more, and you'll foul the tank, possibly killing everything in it. Crayfish will take small pieces of raw meat offered on a wooden skewer, while tadpoles should be given fresh lettuce, washed to remove any trace of pesticides.

Keep the fish and invertebrates no longer than necessary – they are temporary pets. When it comes to releasing them, take them back to their pond, and float the plastic bags for 20 minutes to equalize the temperature, adding pond water a little at a time, before carefully letting them free.

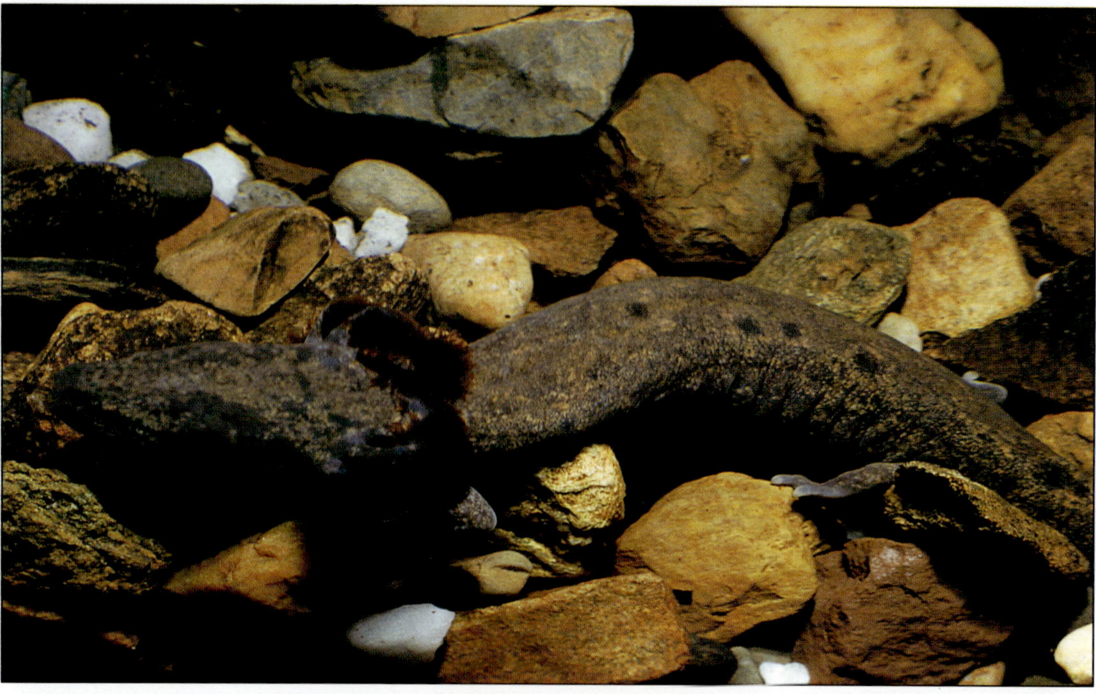

RIGHT Many salamanders start as gilled larvae before becoming air-breathing adults, but the mudpuppy retains its feathery red gills all its life. It can be kept in a well-aerated aquarium, and fed worms and small invertebrates.

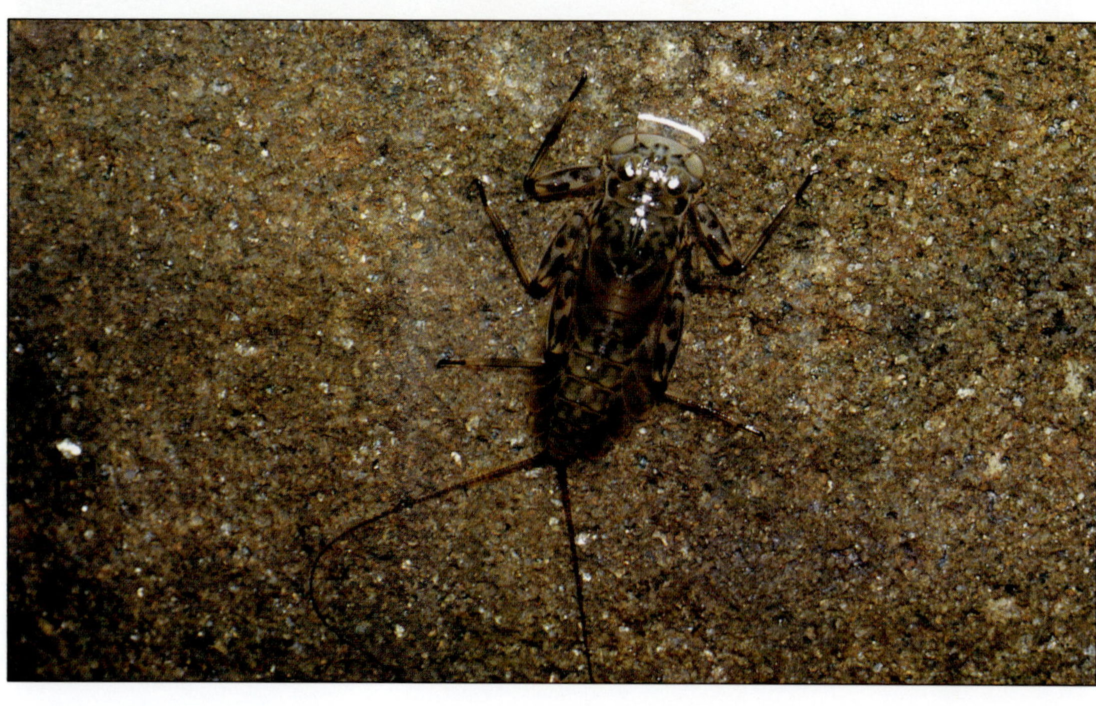

RIGHT Many mayfly larvae, like this *Ephemerella* nymph, require cold, highly oxygenated water to survive, and should not be collected for the home aquarium. Dragonfly or damselfly nymphs from ponds, which tolerate warmer water, are a better choice.

MAKING A GLASS-BOTTOMED BUCKET TO OBSERVE UNDERWATER LIFE

MATERIALS
- 5-gallon plastic bucket
- Circular piece of Plexiglas, cut to size
- Silicone cement

Glass-bottomed viewing boxes have been around for a long time, and provide an excellent way to observe fish and other aquatic life, free from the distortions of ripples and reflections. But traditional models, built of wood and glass, were difficult to make and cumbersome to use. The plastic bucket provides the modern (and cheap) alternative.

Choose the bucket carefully. It should be fairly large (5 gallons is a good size), but most importantly, the bottom must be flat, with no ridges or indentations. Unfortunately, most buckets come with such adornments, so finding the right bucket may be the most time-consuming part of this exercise.

When the correct bucket has been found, measure the inside diameter of the bottom, then use a sharp knife to cut a neat hole with a diameter about 2 inches smaller than the bottom of the bucket; this leaves a 1-inch-wide lip all the way around that serves as a support for the glass.

Actually, a better material than real glass is one of the plastic substitutes, like Plexiglas, which is stronger and less less prone to cracking. Have the hardware store cut a circular piece just slightly smaller than the inside diameter of the bucket. Check for fit.

To seal the window, use a silicone-based glue, such as that used for plumbing or aquarium construction. Apply it liberally, to form a complete seal between the bucket and the Plexiglas; even a small gap will leak. A good technique to avoid such problems is to apply a thick ring of cement on the bucket, about halfway between the hole and where the edge of the window will be. Ease the Plexiglas circle into place, pressing down slightly, then rotate it an inch or two, spreading the glue evenly. Then press the Plexiglas down firmly, weight it lightly to keep it in place, and set it aside to dry according to the directions.

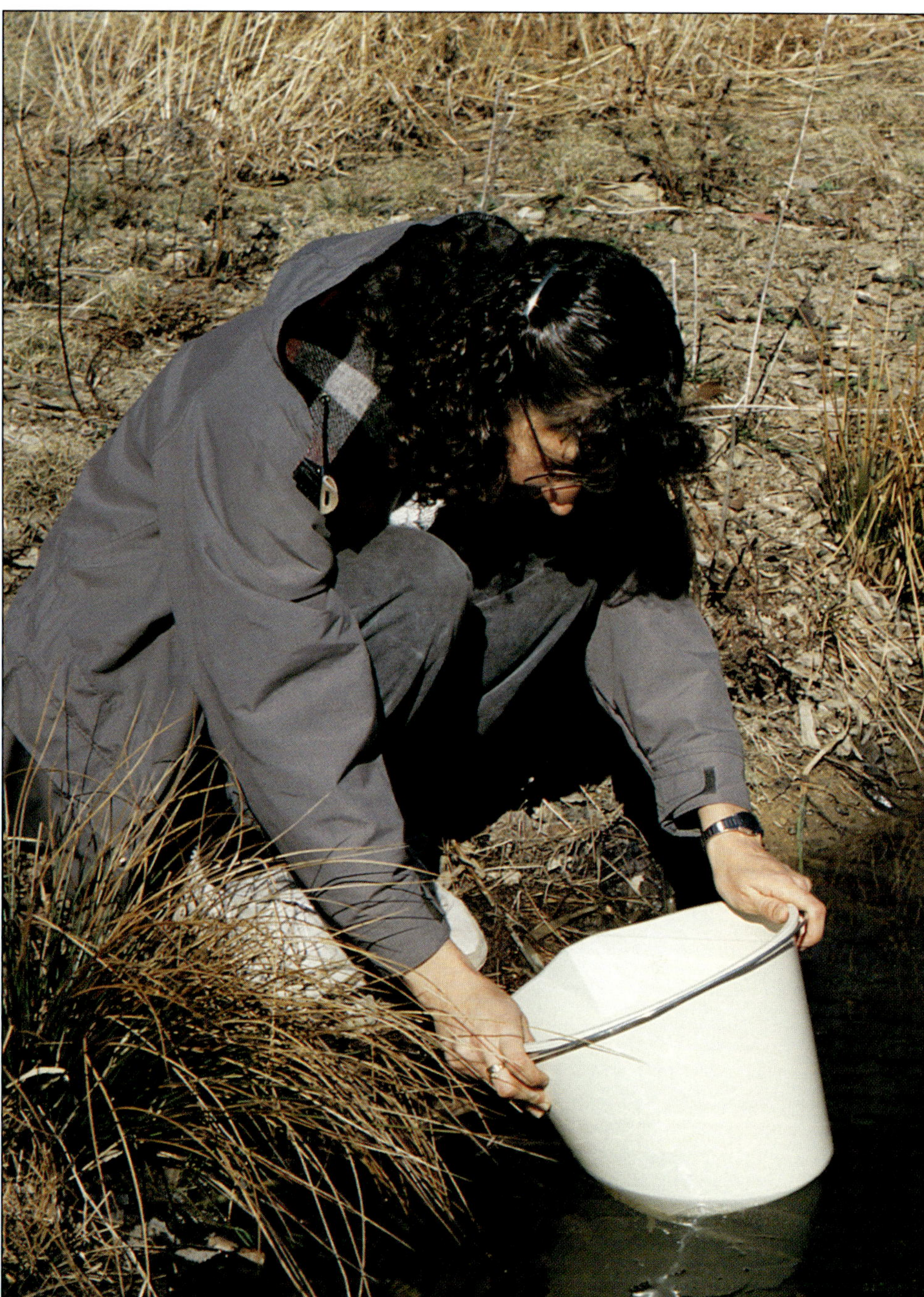

ABOVE By eliminating reflections and surface disturbance, a glass-bottomed bucket allows you to peer beneath the surface of a pond or stream.

COLLECTING MUSHROOM SPORE PRINTS

RECOMMENDED EQUIPMENT

- Colored paper
- Sharp knife
- Large bowls (optional)
- Can of artist's spray fixative

Mycologists – experts in mushrooms and other fungi – frequently rely on the color of the mushroom's spores as a way of identifying these often confusing species. To do so, they make a "spore print" by placing collected mushroom caps on strips of paper.

But in addition to being informative, mushroom spore prints can be delicately beautiful as well. They are easy to make; slice off the stipe (or stalk) of the mushroom as close as possible to the gill surface beneath the cap, using a sharp knife. In the field, the cap can be slipped into a wax-paper bag and then into a field bag, gills up, for temporary storage, but the sooner the print can be made, the better.

Place the cap, gills down, on a sheet of paper. Spore color varies widely, so you will probably want to try several different background tones, looking for the proper combination that will accentuate the spores. Leave the caps overnight, preferably in a quiet, draft-free location; if that is not available, cover the caps with large bowls.

The next morning, gingerly lift away the caps, trying not to disturb the spores that have dropped from the gills. The patterns can be enjoyed for a short time and the paper discarded, or they can be permanently preserved with an aerosol spray fixative, of the sort used by artists to protect charcoal and graphite drawings. Do not spray the print directly, since this will scatter the spores. Instead, shake the can well and spray lightly above the print, allowing the mist of fixative to fall straight down onto the paper. It may take several applications, with a short drying time in between, to completely seal the print.

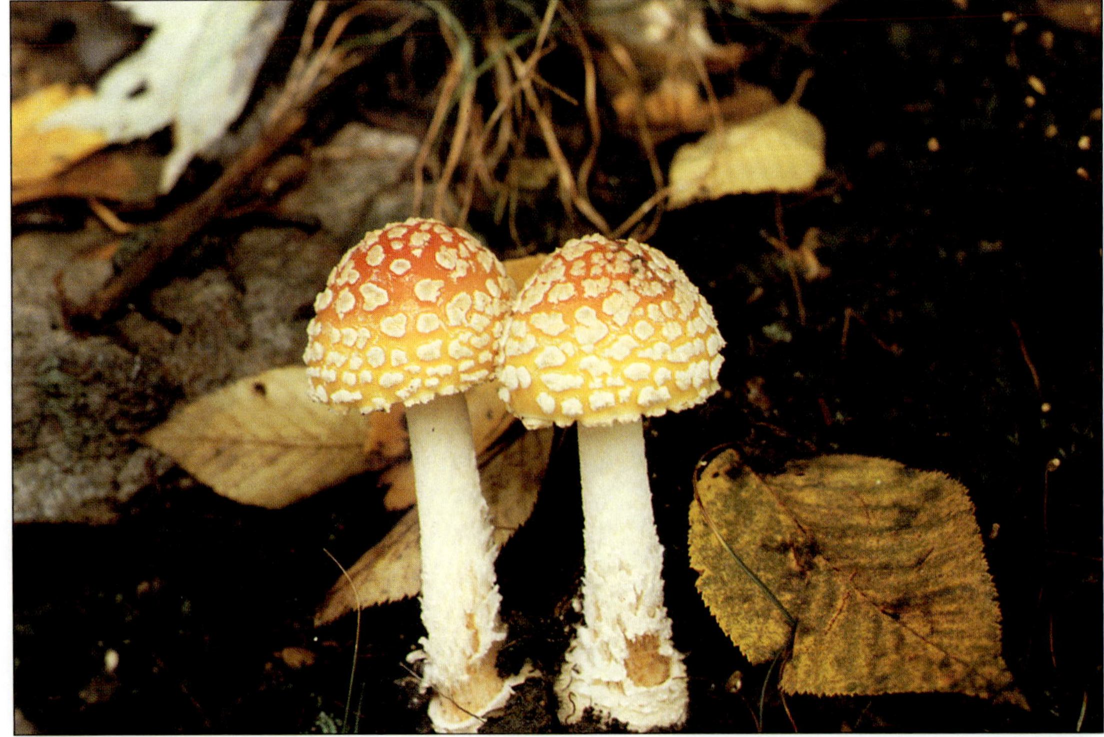

RIGHT Spore prints can be made from almost any capped fungi, but be careful to wash your hands thoroughly after handling unidentified species, since some, like these *Amanitas*, are dangerously poisonous if ingested.

EXPLORING A SUMMER MEADOW

RECOMMENDED EQUIPMENT

- Hand lens
- Binoculars
- Insect, wildflower field guides

Few habitats cram as much life in as small a space as a summertime meadow. Of course, most of the inhabitants are not large, but what they lack in size they more than make up for in interest.

But first, what exactly is a meadow? Not just any old field; a meadow has traditionally been considered grassland that is mown for hay, although today the term encompasses any small, noncultivated field with a wide variety of plant life. It may be an alpine clearing scoured free of trees by an avalanche, and now dotted with a carpet of low-growing flowers, or an old farm field gone wild, filled with black-eyed susans and Queen Anne's lace.

A meadow charms the visitor on several levels. Esthetically, there are the wildflowers for which meadows are best-known. Ironically, many of the species in the East that are most closely associated with meadows – chicory, ox-eye daisies, Queen Anne's lace and orange hawkweed, to name a few – are really alien plants, brought from Europe and now growing in the wild. Still, the natives outnumber the

BELOW Moving slowly through the weeds, the camouflaged praying mantis stalks smaller insects, which it captures with its spiny forelegs.

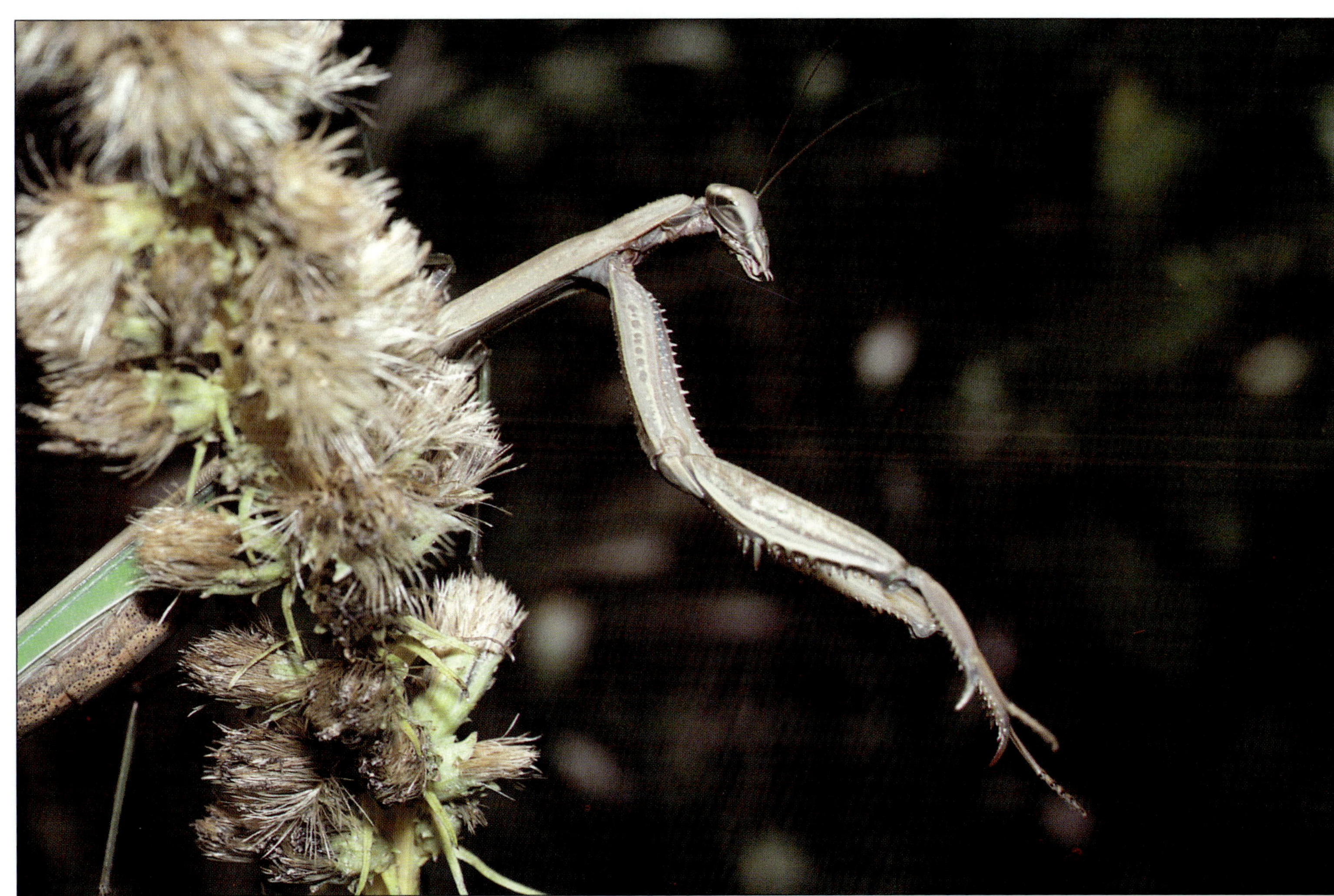

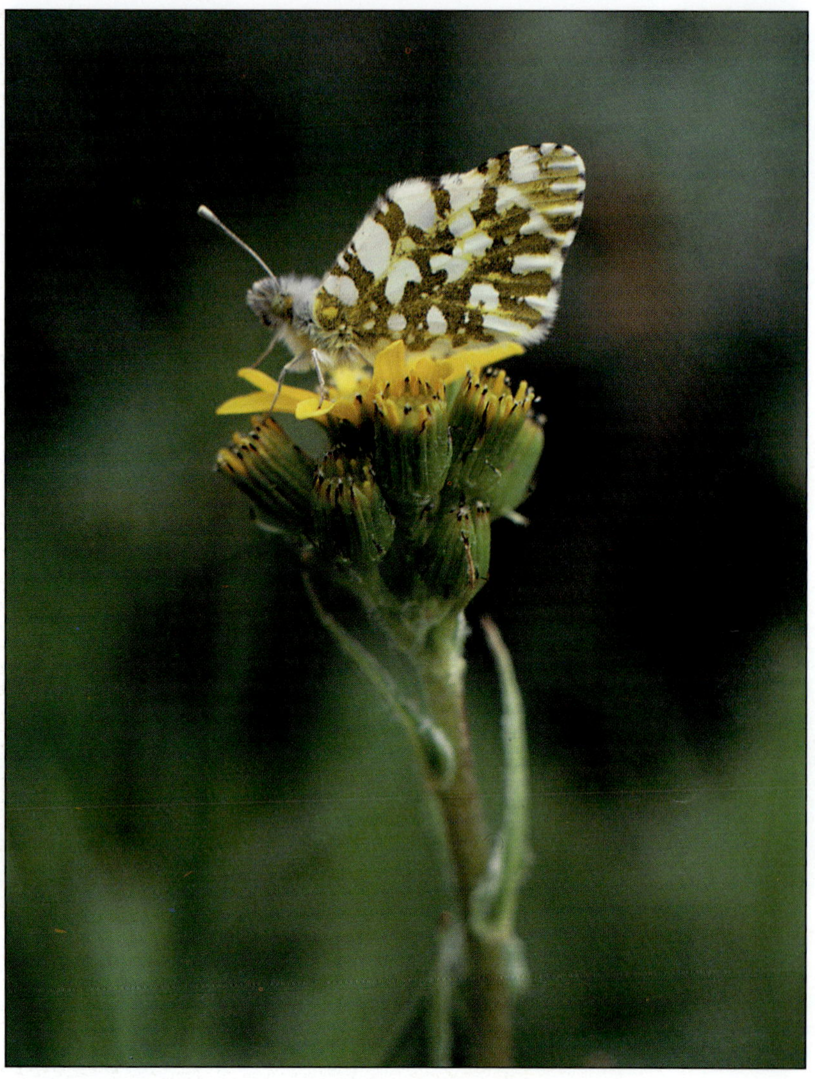

ABOVE In the natural meadows of the Rocky Mountains, wildflowers and butterflies abound.

newcomers, especially the native sunflowers, goldenrods and asters of late summer.

The meadow grasses are also visually pleasing, particularly so on a windy day in mid-summer, when the long blades ripple in the breeze like waves on a lake. Speckled with flowers as a colorful counterpoint to the green, the meadow is a feast for the eye.

But look more closely, for the meadow is alive with insects. Some are obvious at first glance. Butterflies are a fixture of meadows, although only if the sun is shining; should the day turn overcast, they will drop out of sight, roosting beneath leaves and vegetation until the sun returns, warming them sufficiently for flight. Watch their behavior carefully, for butterflies can be as territorial and pugnacious as birds, chasing others of their species from favorite feeding areas. Some are so aggressive that they will attack humans that enter their defended zone – although the attack of a featherweight butterfly is hardly dangerous.

Binoculars, so valuable for bird-watching, can come in handy in the meadow as well. Used normally, they are excellent for observing butterflies and other skittish creatures. Reversed, they function as a make-shift hand lens capable of extreme magnification (see Chapter 2).

There is plenty to see with a hand lens. A single meadow plant may host dozens of different insects and arthropods. Orb spiders, like the large, beautiful black-and-yellow argiope, spin their webs in the corridors between plants, while crab spiders – capable of changing color slowly – hide beneath the flower petals, waiting for flies, bees or butterflies. Soldier beetles, with their orange and black wing covers, feed on the pollen of the goldenrods or asters. On the stem, a glob of froth conceals the larva of the meadow spittlebug, which feeds on the sap of the plant and blows its cluster of bubbles as a defense against predators. Other insects use deception to scare off potential predators. Many of the harmless robber flies and syrphid flies are bee and wasp mimics, matching the bees' color, shape and behavior, but lacking their sting.

The meadow will also hold vertebrates, although not in the same variety as the insects. Voles, shrews, jumping mice, woodchucks, deer mice and weasels live among the tall grass, as do garter, hognose, brown and other snakes. Pickerel frogs – often known as "grass frogs" – may be found far from water, protected from the hot sun by the shade of the meadow plants. The meadow also provides a nesting area for grassland birds, including ring-necked pheasants, upland sandpipers, bobolinks, meadowlarks and others.

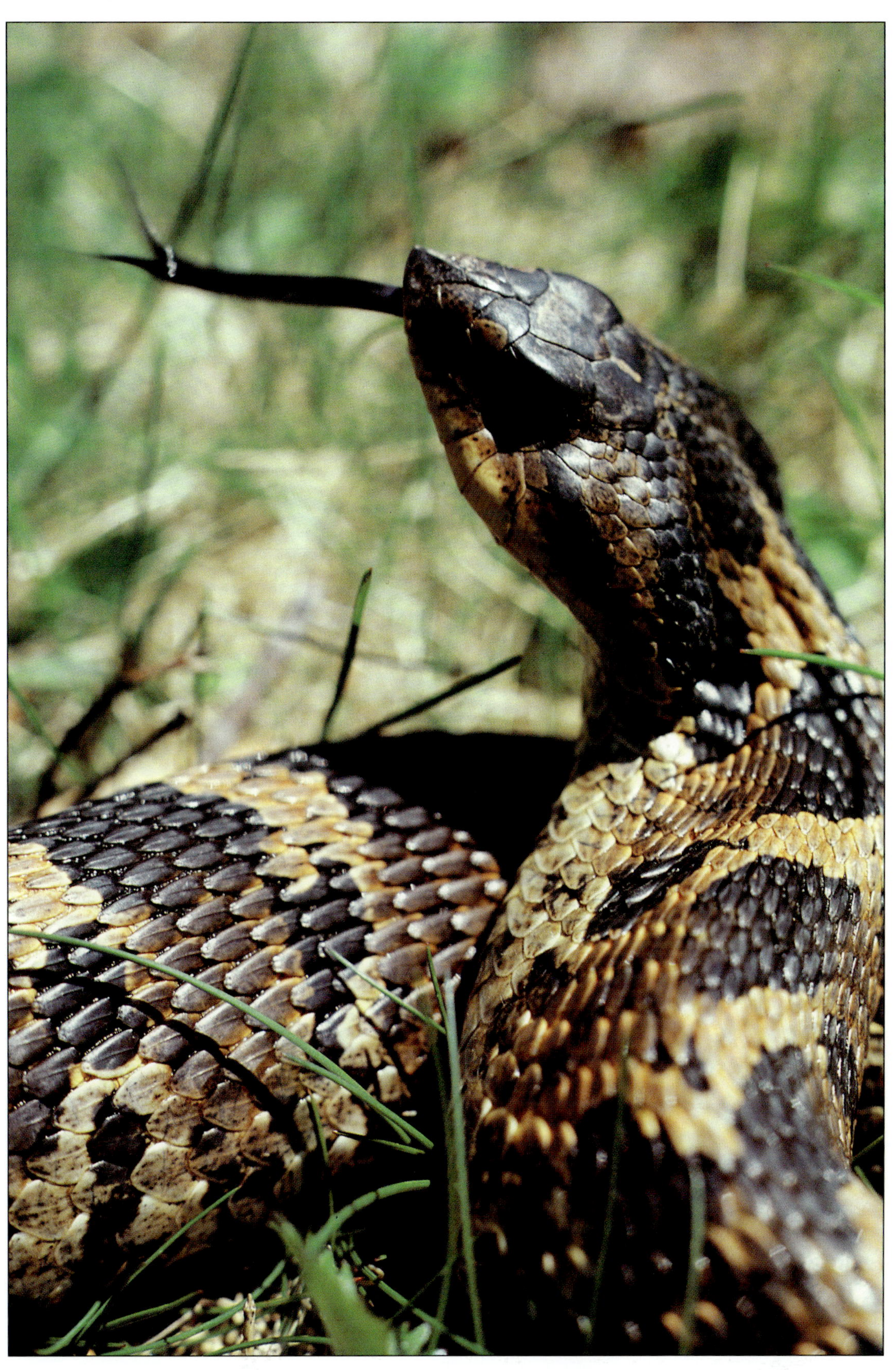

LEFT A harmless resident of meadows and fencerows, the hog-nosed snake is all bluff and no bite; when disturbed it hisses loudly, and may even play dead.

BELOW Among the easiest wildflowers to propagate are the members of the family *Compositae,* which include the sunflowers and asters. This is the green-headed coneflower, *Rudbeckia laciniata.*

RAISING NATIVE WILDFLOWERS FROM SEED

Long ignored in favor of flashy domestic blooms, native wildflowers are increasingly popular among landscapers and home gardeners who want to add a touch of wilderness to their homes.

This growing popularity is two-edged sword, however. Unscrupulous collectors may decimate wild stock to feed the demand, pushing some uncommon species even closer to the brink. Rather than purchasing wildflowers of dubious origins (even the phrase "greenhouse reared" is no guarantee), it is better – and more rewarding – to cultivate your own from seed.

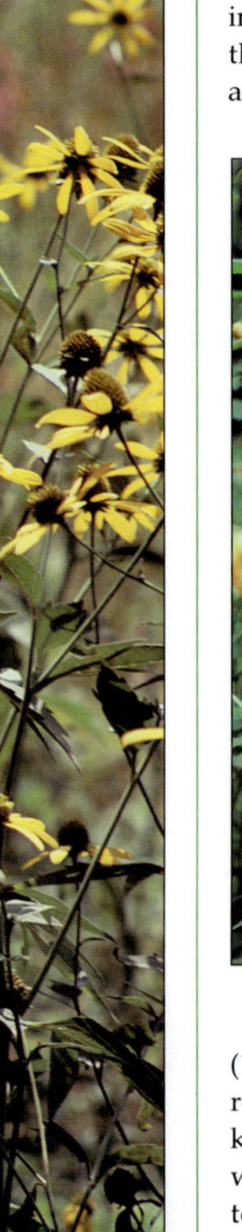

For starters, stick with the common species of meadow flowers, which are relatively easy to propagate – plants like sunflowers (*Helianthus*), black-eyed susans (*Rudbeckia*), coreopsis and butterflyweed (*Asclepias*). Locate and mark the blooming plants; it is remarkable how they disappear into the jumble of meadow grasses once the flowers are finished. When the seeds are ripe, collect some in small plastic bags.

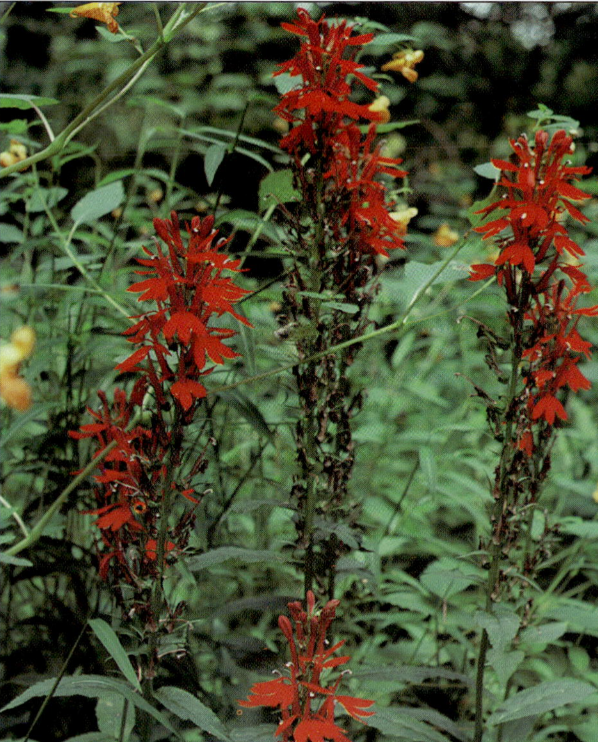

Take only about 20 percent of the seeds (10 percent for rarer species), leaving the rest for natural germination. Obviously, knowing which species are common and which are rare – and which can be expected to do well in the garden – is a prerequisite before collecting; check a field guide if you are in doubt.

LEFT As a general rule, collect no more than 20 percent of the seed from a stand of wildflowers – and in the case of locally uncommon species like the cardinal-flower, *Lobelia cardinalis,* take no more than 5 percent.

RIGHT For wildflowers like violets, which are conspicuous only when they bloom, is is a good idea to mark the plants so you can return when the seeds are ripe.

In most cases, the seeds will need to be exposed to a period of cold, mimicking the winter, before they will germinate. While planted flats of seeds can be left outside during the winter, it is far safer to overwinter seeds in the refrigerator. After collecting the seeds, air-dry them on window screening for several days, then package them, by species, in plastic freezer containers, labeled by name and with collecting information.

Seeds can be sown directly in the ground in the spring, but it is usually safer to plant them in flats, where the chance of destruction from rodents, insects and fungi is reduced. Use a high-quality planting mix, and cover the seeds very lightly. On plastic tags, record the species and date planted.

You may have a long wait. While most species germinate the spring following their bloom, some may wait for two or three years before sprouting, and then grow only very slowly (this is especially true of trilliums and several other woodland wildflowers). Through the growing season, keep the seedlings watered and protected from direct sun, since even plants that grow in brightly lit meadows start out with the shade of the thick surrounding vegetation above them.

When the plants are large enough, they should be transplanted, either to individual pots for further growth, or into the ground. When planting a new species in a wildflower meadow, cluster the plants within the same general area, so that pollinating insects are more likely to transfer pollen among them.

EASY WILDFLOWERS TO GROW FROM SEED

Columbine *(Aquilegia canadensis)*
Collect seeds in late spring or early summer. Overwinter seeds in refrigerated damp sand or paper toweling; sow in spring by scattering seeds on top of planting mix without burying. Do not plant wild columbine near domestic varieties, with which it hybridizes easily.

Butterflyweed *(Asclepias tuberosa)*
Collect seed from pods and trim away down. Overwinter in damp sand in refrigerator.

Coreopsis
Plant immediately after collection; seeds will sprout quickly, and plants can be overwintered in a sheltered location or planted in autumn.

Tickseed sunflower (*Bidens* species)
Plant seeds immediately in fall, or overwinter in refrigerator (overwintered seeds exhibit reduced germination rates). Good for attracting goldfinches.

Black-eyed susans (*Rudbeckia* species)
Sow immediately after collection, transplanting the following summer. Plant where this flower can spread without becoming a pest.

TOP RIGHT Bird-watching can be whatever you want it to be – solitary or social, competitive or reflective, equally enjoyable for the novice or expert.

BOTTOM RIGHT The key to identifying birds is recognizing their field marks – in the case of this great egret, the combination of white plumage, yellow bill and black legs, which separate it from the other five varieties of white wading birds.

BELOW An immature red-tailed hawk watches for mice from a telephone pole. Many birders specialize in watching raptors, while others prefer songbirds, waterfowl or shorebirds.

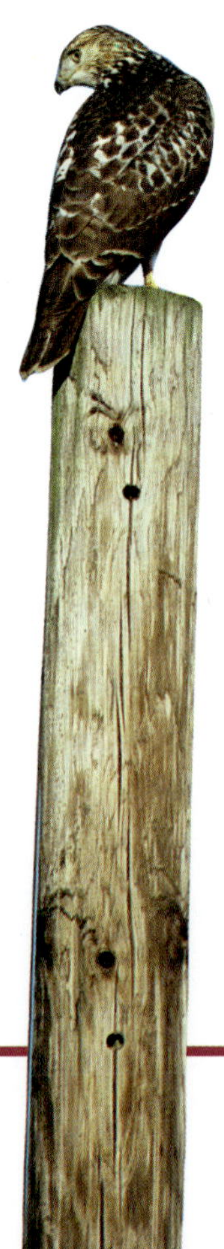

INTRODUCTION TO BIRD-WATCHING

Bird-watching is perhaps the fastest-growing outdoor pastime in North America. Once considered the hobby of eccentrics, it has become completely mainstream – and with good reason. Bird-watching is fun.

More than 800 species of birds can be found within the confines of North America, either as regular breeders, migrants or wayward wanderers. The sheer variety can be daunting to a beginner thumbing through a field guide, but it should not be. There's no need to learn every bird – concentrate on those found in your region, and start only with the most common of those species.

The equipment for birding (as it is now most often known) is very simple – a good field guide and a pair of binoculars. Buy the best binoculars you can afford, because the aggravation of using poor optics outweighs the financial savings. For general birding, 7-power glasses have traditionally been considered standard, although more and more birders are using 8-power for songbirds, and up to 10-power for shorebirds, waterfowl and raptors.

There are a large number of field guides to the birds on the market, but all function on the principle of field marks, laid out with the publication of the first comprehensive guide in 1934, Roger Tory Peterson's *A Field Guide to the Birds*, fully revised and still one of the best. Field marks, simply put, are colors, patterns, shapes and behaviors that are characteristic for each species, and which allow identification at a distance. The red breast of a robin is a field mark, as are the spotted breast and bobbing tail of the spotted sandpiper. Each species has a unique set of field marks that distinguish it from similar birds.

The beauty of birding is that it can be enjoyed anywhere. Even big cities (especially those with wooded parks) offer surprisingly good opportunities. Furthermore, the players change with the shifting seasons – neotropical migrants flooding

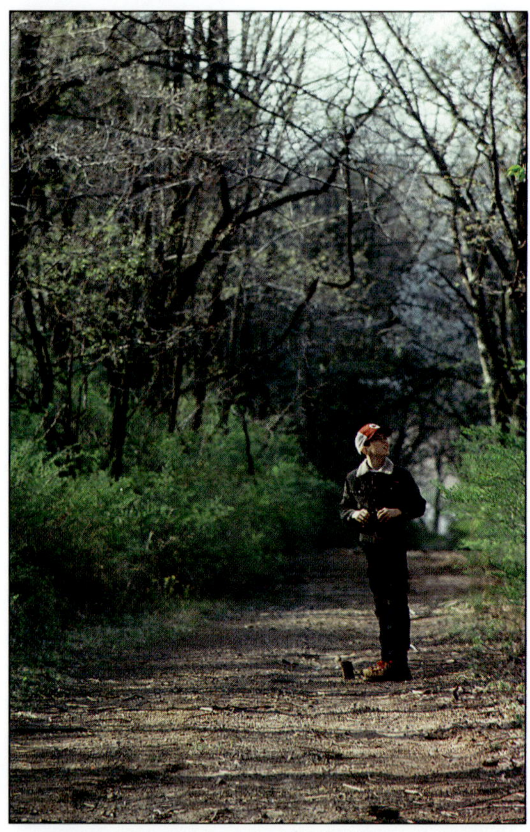

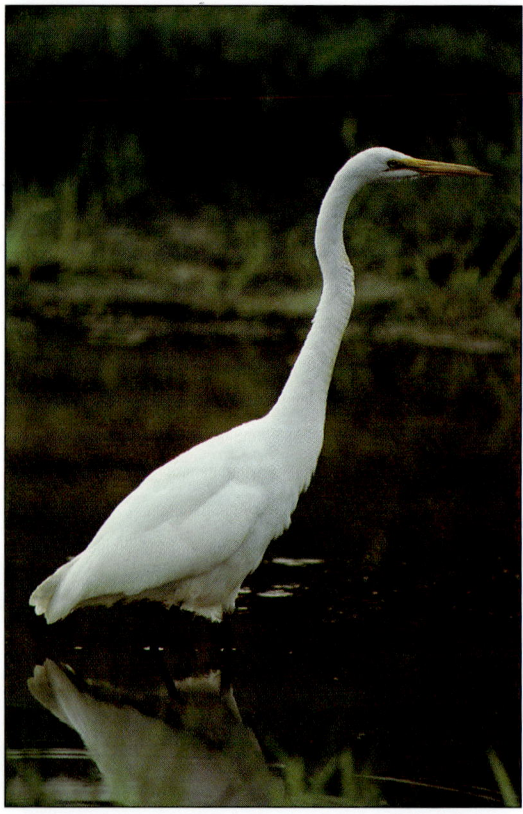

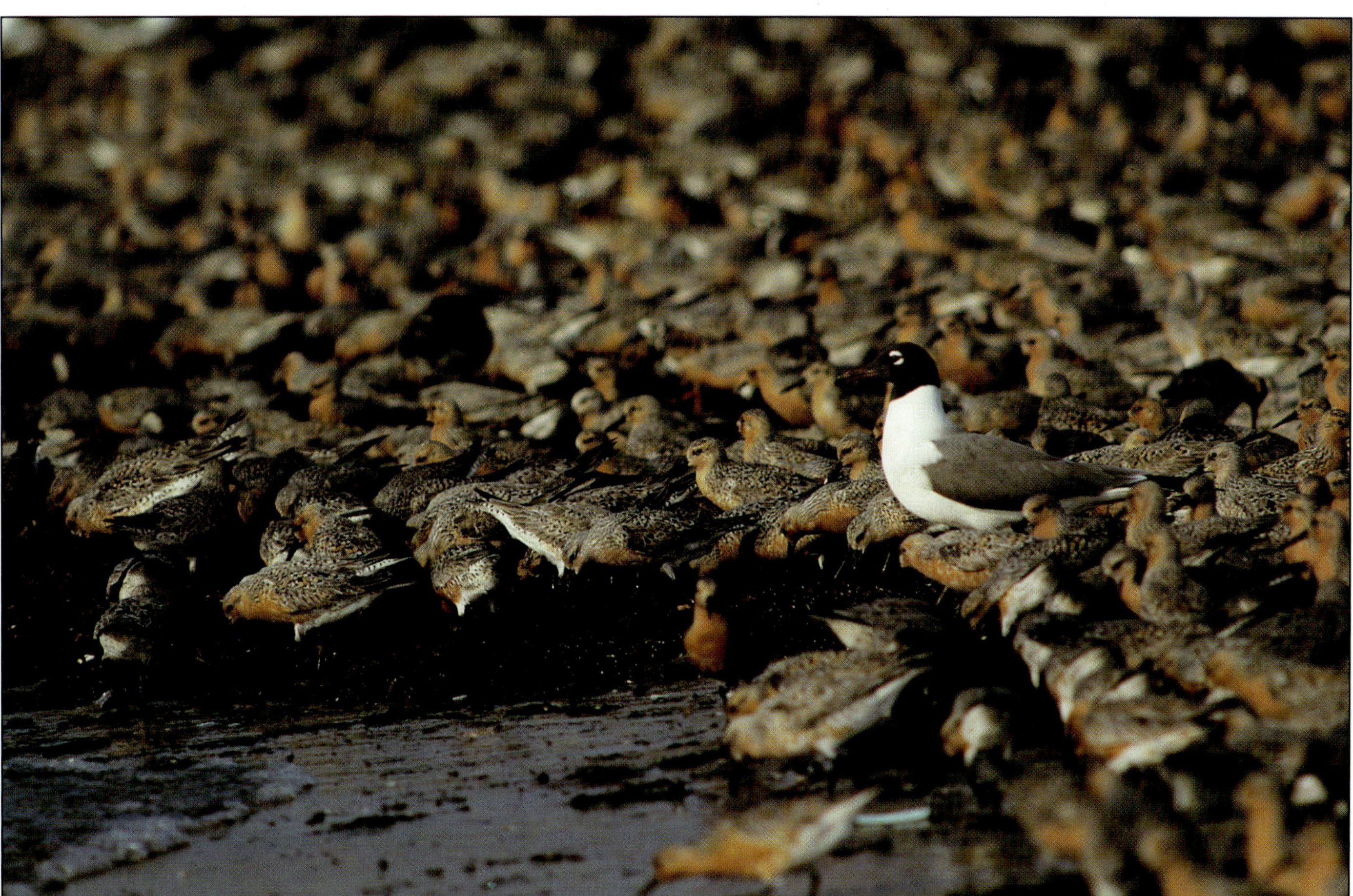

north in the spring, winter finches and arctic raptors invading south from Canada in the winter, strays blown off course by autumn storms. The same piece of real estate rarely hosts exactly the same birdlife from visit to visit, and the chance of discovery is one of the hobby's biggest thrills.

Bird-watching's limits may be few, but there are some pointers that make it even more rewarding. Early morning is by far the best time to be afield, especially during the spring and summer breeding season, when the birds are at their most active. Males sing from the boundaries of their territories, while females gather nesting materials and food for the nestlings. Later, during the autumn migration, flocks of songbirds may literally fill the trees, exhausted after a night of long-distance flying on their way south.

Each habitat has a different cast of players, so the richest birding will come where two or more habitats meet – what biologists refer to as an "ecotone," or edge habitat. This may be a meadow set in a hardwood forest, brushy fencerows running through grassland, or marshes at the verge of a woodland lake.

Good birders also use their ears as much as their eyes – in some cases, even more. Songs, call notes and even mechanical sounds, like the whistle of wings, can provide identification clues, and in some groups – like the flycatchers – song may be the only way to separate two similar species. Listen to recordings of birds in your region, trying to learn the rhythm, melody and tone of the song. It helps to use a mnemonic approach, applying words to the song as a memory aid; the song of the olive-sided flycatcher is usually written as *Hic-three-beers*, for example.

ABOVE Hundreds of red knots surround a laughing gull as they feed on horseshoe crab eggs along the Delaware Bay. Coastal areas are rich in birdlife, and exciting for birders.

RIGHT Each kind of seed attracts a different variety of birds – from left, white proso millet, niger (or "thistle") seed, cracked corn, oil sunflower seed and peanut hearts.

BELOW A flat tray feeder works best for larger songbirds, like these evening grosbeaks feeding on sunflower seeds.

SETTING UP A BIRD-FEEDING STATION

RECOMMENDED EQUIPMENT

- Tube feeder
- Suet feeder and suet
- Black sunflower seed
- Plastic squirrel guard (if needed)

Feeding birds in the winter is satisfying in several ways. Altruistically, it feels good to help another living thing get through the hardest part of the year. At the same time, the birds provide us with a distraction from the dreary weather – a splash of color and excitement through the long months. It is a pretty good deal for all concerned.

Setting up a feeding station is not complicated or overly expensive. More important than the price of the feeders is that you match the type of food to the sorts of birds you see nearby, and present it in the proper setting.

Songbirds live their lives in a state of barely subdued alarm, ready to bolt at the appearance of a hawk, cat, weasel or other

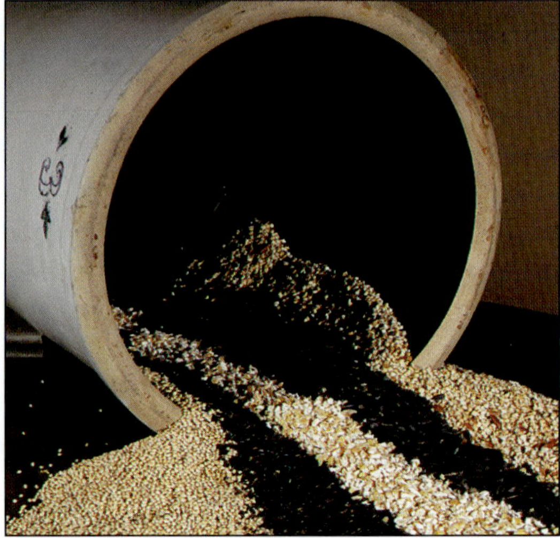

predator. For that reason, a good feeding station should provide escape cover close at hand – a bush, tree, hedge or thicket into which the birds can dive if they are attacked. A feeding station in a spot without escape cover (such as a new housing development not yet landscaped) will attract little, if anything. Before you start hanging feeders, pick the location carefully, taking advantage of the vegetation around the house (and bearing in mind that autumn, when most feeders go up, is a great time to plant shrubs for additional

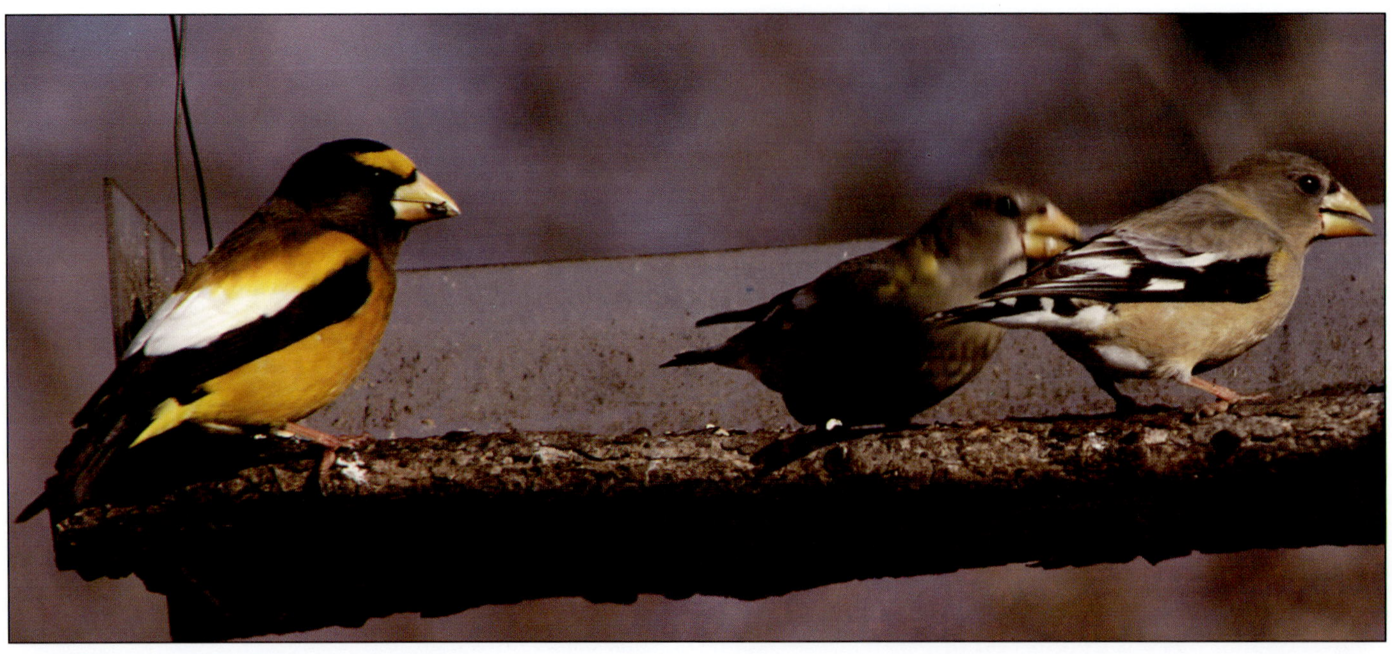

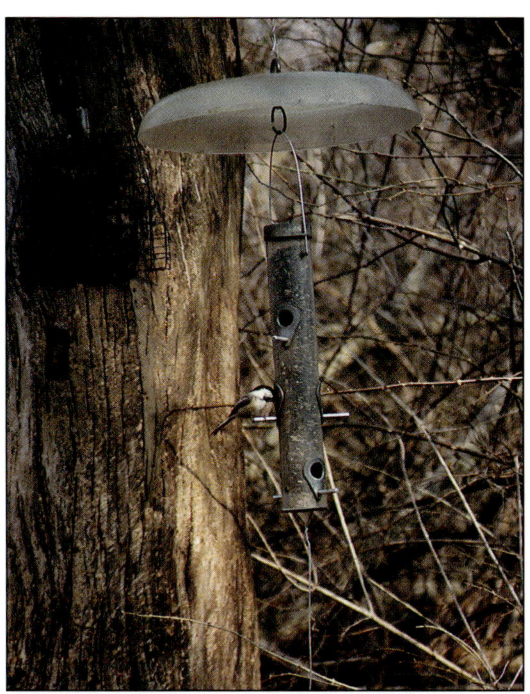

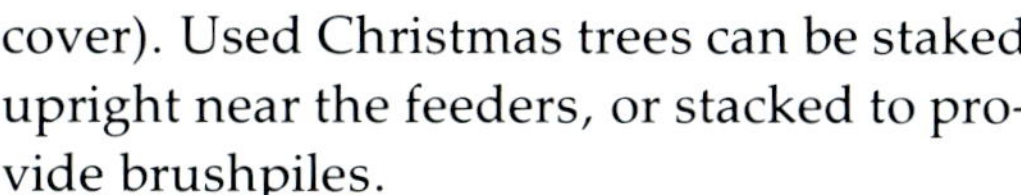

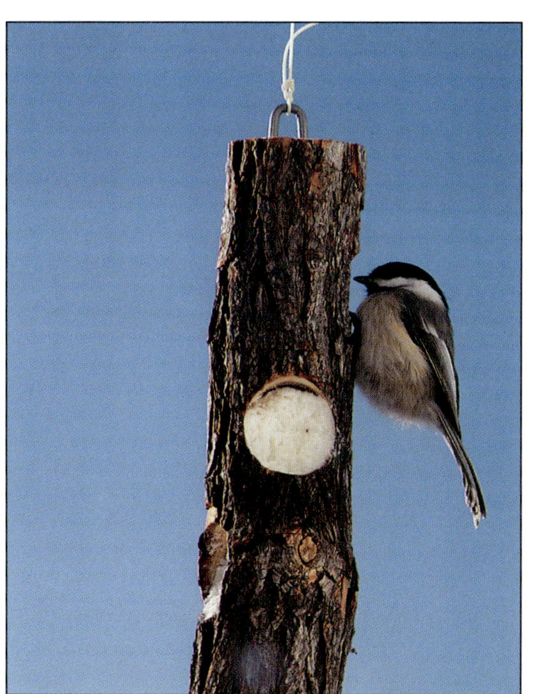

FAR LEFT A plastic squirrel baffle like this is effective only if the feeder is hung far from the tree trunk – otherwise the squirrels will simply jump to the tube.

LEFT An inexpensive suet feeder can be made from a section of tree branch, cut to length, with several one-inch-wide holes drilled into it.

cover). Used Christmas trees can be staked upright near the feeders, or stacked to provide brushpiles.

Far and away the best food is black (or "oil") sunflower seed, a smaller, more nutritious variety than the common striped-hull seed. More species of birds will eat oil sunflower than any other single food; it is small enough for diminutive birds like pine siskins and goldfinches, but attractive to larger grosbeaks and cardinals as well.

For ground-feeders like juncos, sparrows and doves, finely cracked corn or white millet are good alternative choices. Woodpeckers, chickadees and nuthatches enjoy suet (beef fat), while peanuts – shelled or whole – are taken by blue jays. Avoid feeding bread, which attracts pest birds like starlings, and has little nutritional value.

Feeders come in many shapes and sizes, each suited to a particular situation. Plastic tube feeders, designed to hold sunflower seed, are good for small birds, but discourage larger species that can't land on the tiny perches. The same is true of plastic bowl feeders. Tray feeders (often with a roof or food hopper) are the most generalized design, and will handle almost any species; they are vulnerable to squirrels and starlings, however. A dish-shaped squirrel baffle may be of some help, although squirrels are famous for their tenacity and ingenuity in getting around barriers.

Suet should be hung in wire boxes (the metal should be coated by the manufacturer to prevent a bird's feet or eye from freezing fast in frigid weather). Many birds prefer no feeder at all, and if rodents will not be a problem, it is a good idea to simply toss seed on the ground below the feeder.

While most people feed only in the winter, there is no compelling reason to stop in warm weather, although suet should be removed since it will spoil. Be sure to keep the feeders clean, especially in humid climates, to prevent the spread of disease. Washing the feeders with hot water (no soap) once a week is advisable.

Water can be as great an attractant as food, although it is harder to provide in the winter months. Traditional concrete bird baths are hard to keep clean; a better choice are modern plastic models with lift-out bowls that can be washed every few days. For winter use, electric immersion heaters keep the water just above freezing.

BUILDING AND PLACING BIRDBOXES

Most birds build cuplike nests in the open, on tree branches, in bushes or on the ground. But some birds – the cavity nesters – take over holes in trees for their nest sites.

Unfortunately, a suitable cavity can be hard to find. Increasingly, standing dead timber is cut for firewood, or in the mistaken belief that it is useless to the forest community. Those cavities that do remain may have holes large enough to admit raccoons and other predators. Even if a bird finds just the right hole, it may be chased out by an aggressive, alien species like the house sparrow or European starling.

Artificial nest boxes are a partial answer. Built to precise specifications and erected in the right habitat, they can go a long way toward filling the need for nest cavities.

The bird that has benefited the most from nest boxes has been the eastern bluebird. Once one of the most common country birds, it suffered from the loss of nest sites and competition from sparrows and starlings. In some regions, the sight of a bluebird became a rare occurrence by the 1960s. Fortunately, bluebirds take readily to wooden nest boxes, and those with a 1½-inch entrance hole allow the bluebirds to enter, but keep out the bigger starlings. Organizations and individuals across the U.S. and Canada have built and erected millions of bluebird boxes over the past several decades, and the results have been spectacular. The bluebird is again common in many areas, thanks to human intervention.

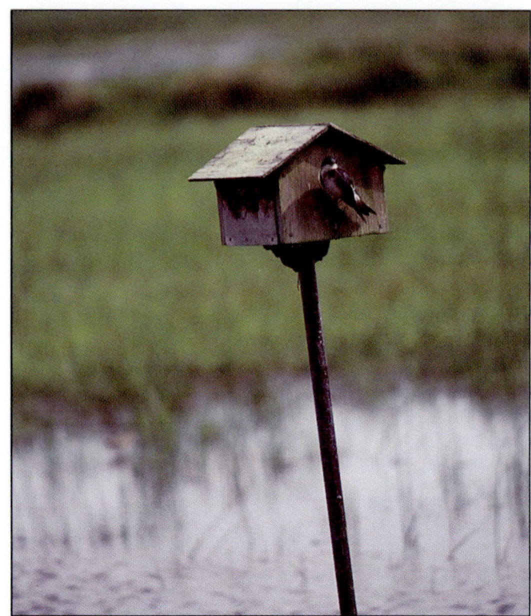

RIGHT The best results come by tailoring nestbox design and placement for a specific species, like this tree swallow box erected over a shallow lake . . .

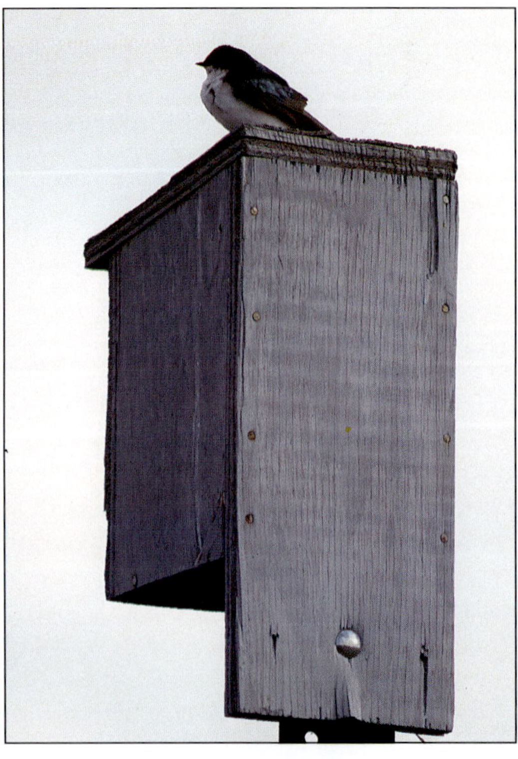

. . . but a generalized design may also work – this tree swallow has taken over a bluebird box along a country road (RIGHT).

The list of birds that nest in artificial boxes is long, and includes more than just songbirds. Wood ducks, for example, are another nest-box success story; in many parts of the Northeast, the population of wood ducks is limited almost exclusively by the availability of nesting sites, and a string of appropriately sized boxes along a stream or river can increase the local flock quickly. The same box may also play host to a family of common or hooded mergansers, two other cavity-nesting ducks.

Large boxes will attract screech-owls, saw-whet owls and barred owls in the woods and American kestrels in farmland. Tall, narrow boxes tightly packed with sawdust are suitable for flickers, which need to "excavate" a cavity even in an artificial site. A long, horizontal box, nailed to the inside of a barn and with an entrance hole cut through the barn wall, will attract mice-eating barn owls. Among the smaller birds that accept boxes are house wrens, tree swallows, great crested flycatchers, chickadees, titmice and nuthatches. Obviously, the potential is tremendous.

Plans for a basic nest box are given on the following page, along with measurements for each group of species. There are some general guidelines that apply to almost all boxes, however. Use wood, preferably ¾-inch, which provides superior protection from heat and cold; do not use pressure-treated, preserved wood, however, since the vapors given off by the preservative are dangerous. Instead, use an oil-based stain, or leave the box untreated.

Build the box with a hinged side or roof so it can be cleaned at the end of the nesting season – an important bit of maintenance. Be sure to drill several large drainage holes in the bottom, because wind-driven rain can fill a small box quickly, drowning the chicks. Lastly, never put a perch on a bird box – the nesting birds do not need it, and it provides a place for starlings or sparrows to land to harass the owners.

Placement is as important as construction. Bluebird boxes should be erected on fenceposts or their own pole, about chest-high in the open. Face the box south or east, away from prevailing winds, and if possible place it so a tree or shrub is 10 or 15 feet from the front – a perch for the fledglings' first flight. Barred owl boxes should be mounted 20–30 feet high in moist hardwood forests, while kestrel boxes should be the same height on an isolated tree, post or the back of a billboard. Wood duck boxes can be erected on trees that border streams, rivers and wooded lakes, but better predator protection is provided by driving a post into shallow water, mounting the box about five feet above the surface, and placing a metal sleeve around the exposed post to keep raccoons away.

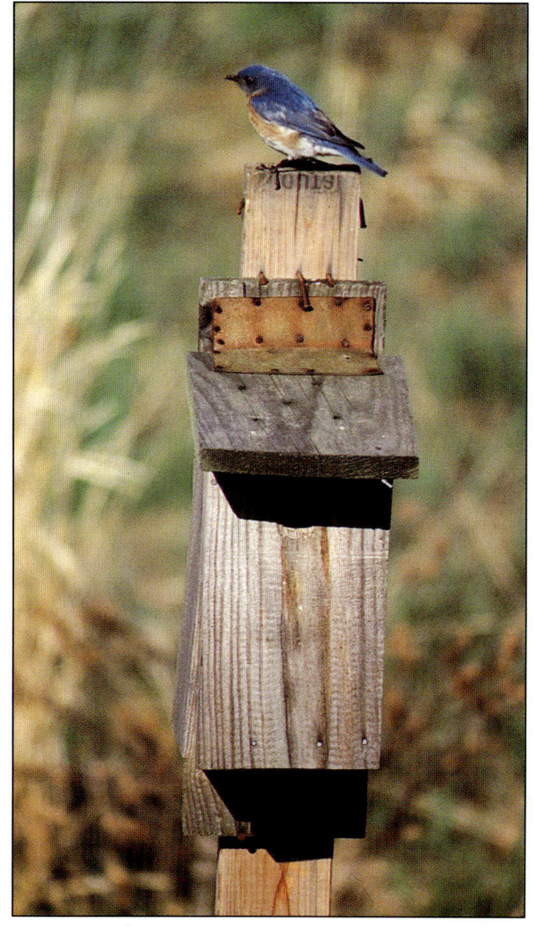

LEFT Plain, unfinished wood provides excellent insulation and a natural appearance; for this bluebird box, a leather strip serves as a hinge for the roof.

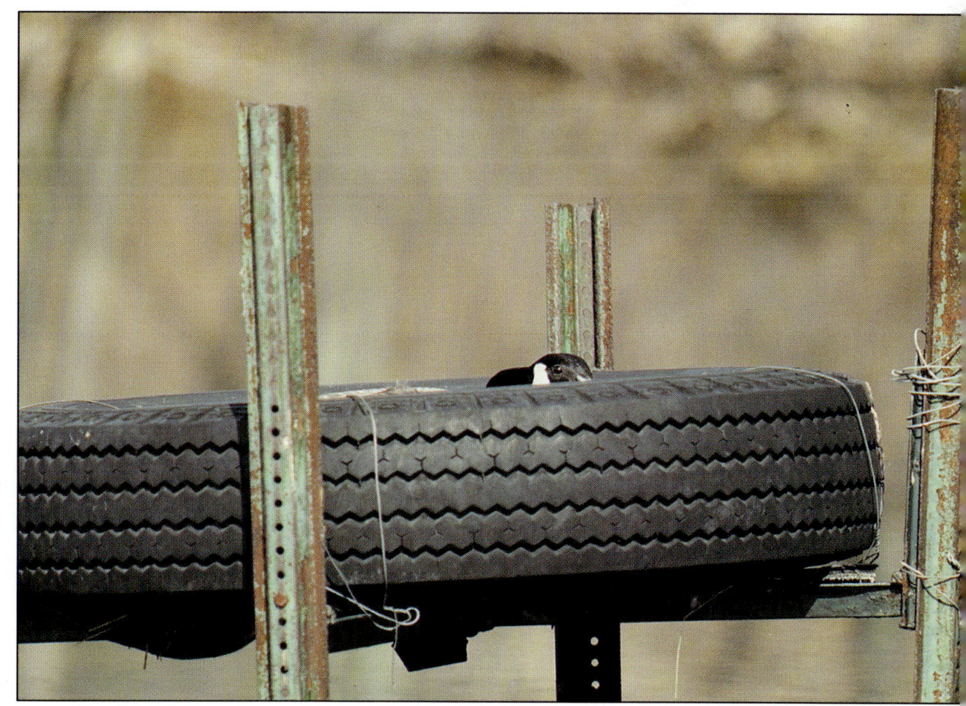

BELOW Not all artificial nest structures are boxes. An old truck tire, fitted with a mesh floor and erected on a platform in a marsh, gives Canada geese a place to nest out of the reach of raccoons.

BIRDBOX PLANS

The plans given here are for a basic nest box of the sort used for bluebirds, but by modifying the proportions in accordance with the chart, you can adapt this design for a wide variety of birds and mammals. See the section on building nest boxes for more information about materials (see page 40).

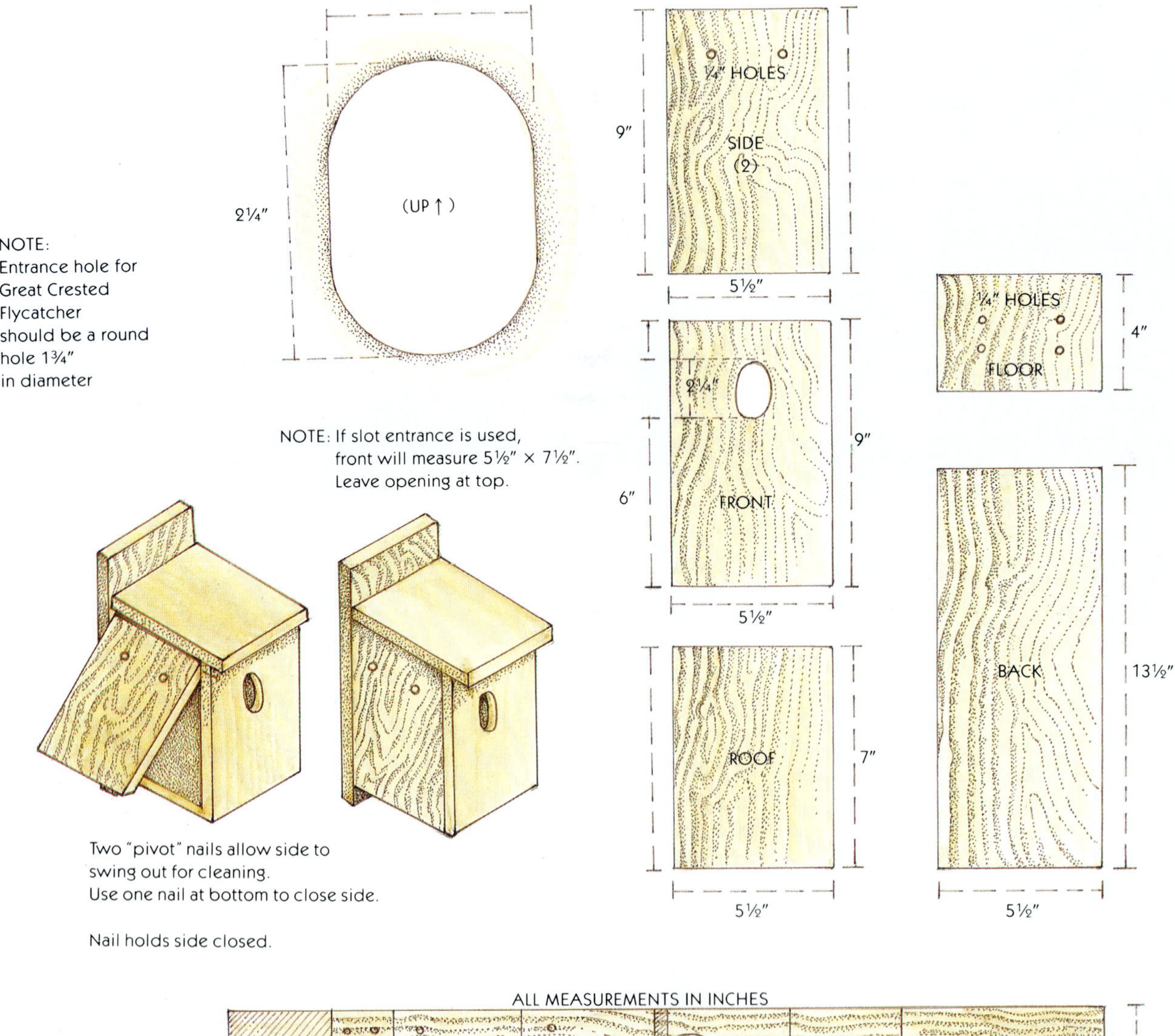

Plans and measurements adapted from *Woodworking for Wildlife,* with permission from Pennsylvania Wild Resource Conservation Fund.

SPECIES	OVERALL SIZE (HEIGHT, WIDTH, DEPTH)	ENTRANCE HOLE	NOTES
E. bluebird Tree swallow Great crested flycatcher	9 × 5½ × 4	1½	Flycatcher hole should be 1¾.
House wren Tufted titmouse White-breasted nuthatch Prothonotary warbler	8 × 5½ × 4	1¼	
N. flicker	24 × 7¼ × 4½	2½	Pack with sawdust to roof.
Barn owl	16 × 40 × 12	7 square	Mount lengthwise on interior barn ledge.
Barred owl	23 × 13 × 12¼	7 square	Entrance hole on side of box.
Am. kestrel E. screech-owl N. saw-whet owl	16 × 19¼ × 7¾	3	2″ wood shavings in bottom of box.
Wood duck Hooded merganser Common merganser Raccoon Gray squirrel Pileated woodpecker	24 × 11¼ × 9¾	3 × 4 oval 5 × 9 oval 3 round 4 round	Wire screening on inside front so chicks can climb out. Fill to roof with sawdust.

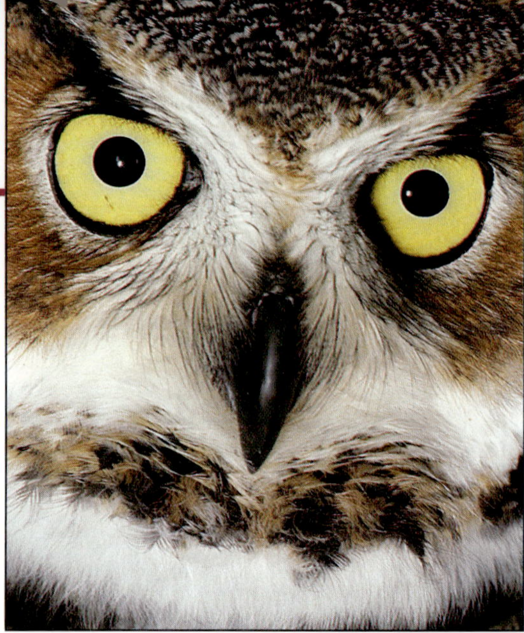

RIGHT Great horned owls are the largest species of owl over most of North America, and respond well to imitations of their deep, seven-noted hoots.

"OWLING"

RECOMMENDED EQUIPMENT
- Portable tape player
- Tape recording of owl calls
- Flashlight

Owls are among the most mysterious of birds, with their sepulcher calls and night-roaming habits. Although fairly common in most areas, they are rarely seen, even by ardent bird-watchers. There is a way to observe owls, however, often at very close range. Known as "owling," it involves the use of tape recordings of owl calls.

Not all owls respond well to tapes of their own vocalizations. Fortunately, the most responsive are also the most widespread – the great horned owl, the eastern and western screech-owls, the barred owl and the northern saw-whet owl.

One important caution: Do not play tapes during the breeding season, which for owls runs from January through early summer. To do so will disrupt the pair's activities, and may even lead to them abandoning their territory or nest. Late fall and early winter are best for owling.

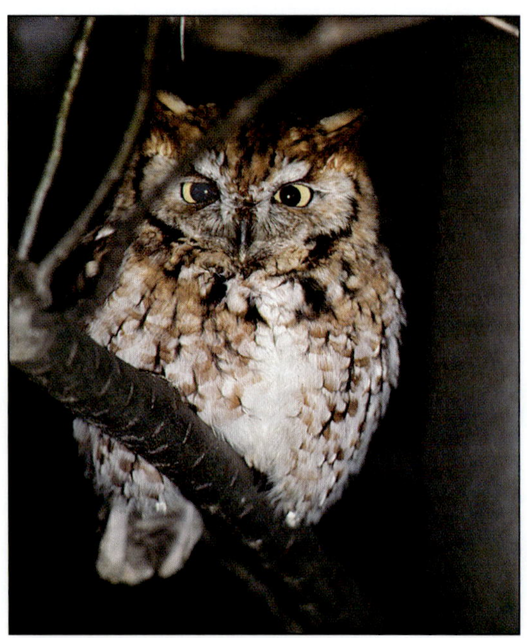

RIGHT Exercise restraint when using the tape recorded calls of any owl, such as the eastern screech-owl. In particular, never use tapes during the breeding season, when it may interfere with courtship or nesting.

Check field guides for the commonest species in your area. Habitat is also important; great horned owls and eastern screech-owls are most common in deciduous forests and woodlots, while barred owls prefer swamps, moist woods and, in the West, coniferous forests. Look for western screech-owls along waterways and in oak forests, and for the tiny saw-whet owl in coniferous and mixed woods, thickets and bogs.

While it is possible to buy specially made owling tapes, most birders simply record the calls from bird song identification records (see reference section). Record each species several times, so that you have a minute or two of uninterrupted calls.

Owls may respond to calls at any time of the day or night (barred owls in particular are famous for daylight calling), but the most effective times are on still, moonlit nights, after midnight; the last hour or two before dawn are exceptionally good. Start with the calls of the smallest species first, because the hoots of a great horned or barred owl may scare the tinier birds (which are frequently eaten by their larger cousins) into silence. Play the tape at medium volume for 30 seconds or so, then listen for a response. Watch the sky, if possible, for the silhouette of the owl flying in to land in nearby trees. Screech and saw-whet owls are quite tame, and will often tolerate a flashlight beam, but the larger owls are more skittish.

COLLECTING AND ANALYZING OWL PELLETS

RECOMMENDED EQUIPMENT

- Plastic bags
- Mothballs (for storing pellets)

Owls are messy eaters. Unlike hawks, which often daintily pluck their prey, owls wrench off large chunks that are eaten bones, fur, feathers and all. Smaller prey items may simply be swallowed whole.

The roughage is indigestible, and although it plays a valuable role in cleaning the stomach, the owl must eventually rid itself of this unwanted material. It does so,

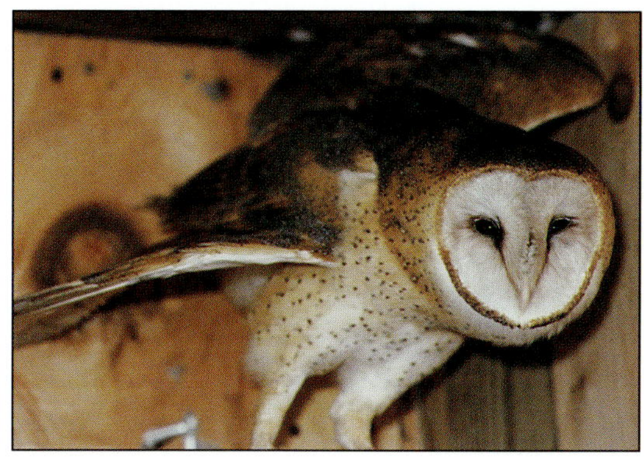

a number of hours after eating, by regurgitating a pellet – a tightly wound mass of fur and bones.

Such pellets have proven invaluable to biologists researching the food habits of owls. Remains of virtually everything the owl eats show up in the pellets, including the chitinous shells of insects; only soft prey, like earthworms, leave no trace. Pellets are exceptionally useful since owls, being nocturnal, are so difficult to observe in the wild.

Pellets are easy to find, especially in late winter just after the snow has melted, revealing a season's worth. Search dense groves of evergreens (a favorite winter roost location), or at the base of large hardwoods where owls have been seen. Barns, silos and old buildings are favored haunts of barn owls. The pellets are usually cast while the owl is on its daytime roost, so you'll probably find a large number in a fairly small area. Although wet when first cast, the pellets quickly dry, and are not at all unpleasant to handle.

Back home, carefully pull apart the pellets, separating the bones from the fur or feathers; it may help to soak the pellet in warm water first. Generally speaking, each pellet represents one meal, and most will probably contain rodent remains. Remarkably, the delicate skull usually survives intact, offering the best method of identifying the prey; consult a field guide to mammals, or a collection of skulls at a local museum.

The remains of larger prey may be fragmented and harder to identify, but comparing the size and shape of bone fragments to a skeletal collection will allow at least tentative identification. Cleaned bones present no storage problems, but whole pellets should be kept with mothballs to prevent insect infestation.

LEFT The pellets of barn owls can often be found in old buildings and silos, where the owls roost and nest.

BELOW A dissected barn owl pellet reveals the bones of a short-tailed shrew (left) and a rat.

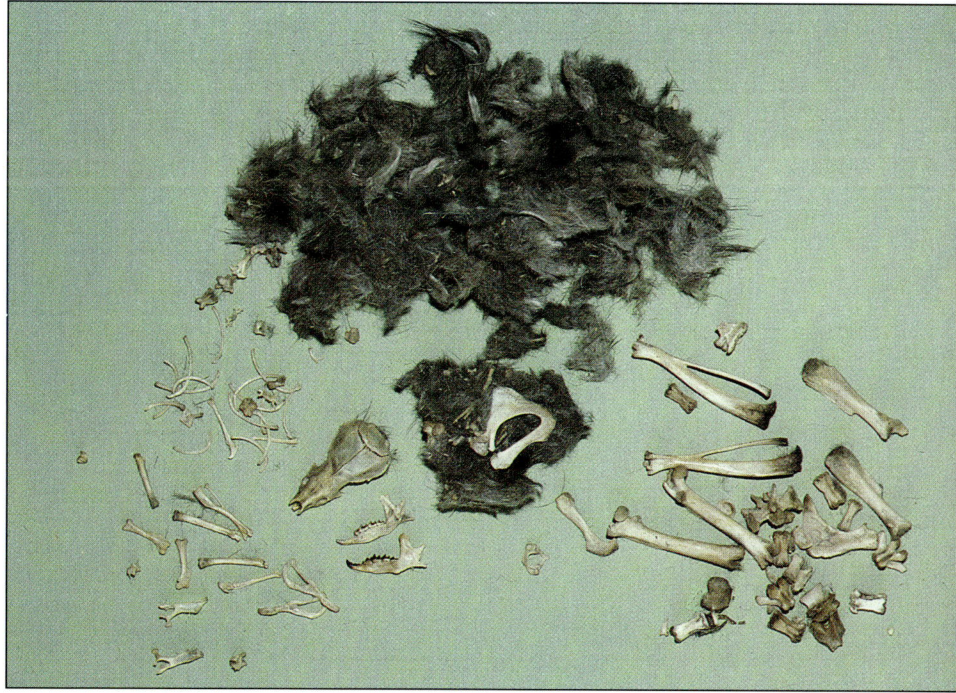

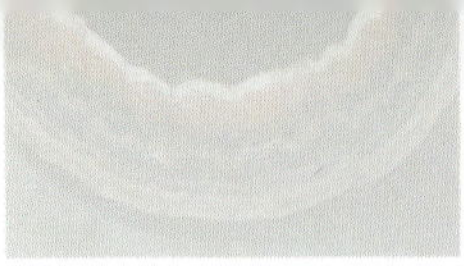

EXPLORING THE NIGHTTIME MARSH BY FLASHLIGHT

RECOMMENDED EQUIPMENT

- Hip boots, waders or substitute
- Flashlight (with detachable red filter)
- Hand lens
- Small dip net and bucket, if desired

When the sun goes down, darkness transforms the marsh from a simple expanse of shallow water and emergent vegetation into a mysterious world of strange sounds and sights. Exploring the marsh at night, by flashlight, is to enter that mysterious world.

Hip boots or chest waders are the ideal footwear, providing waterproofing and

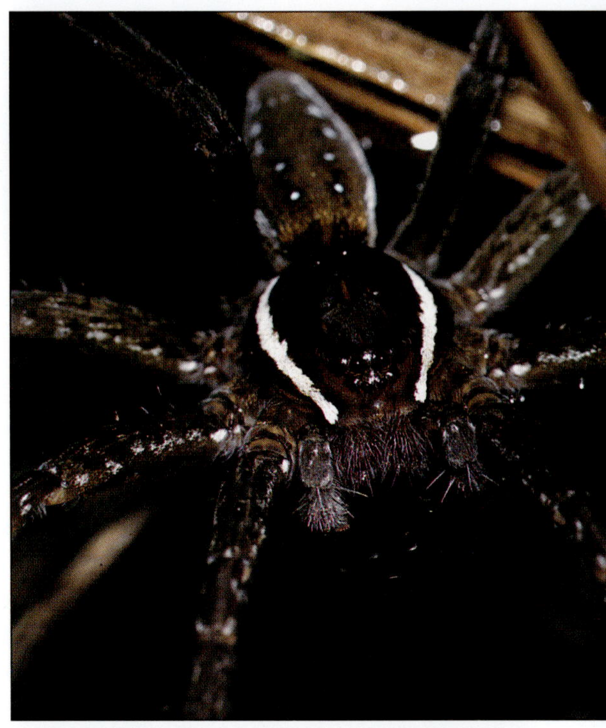

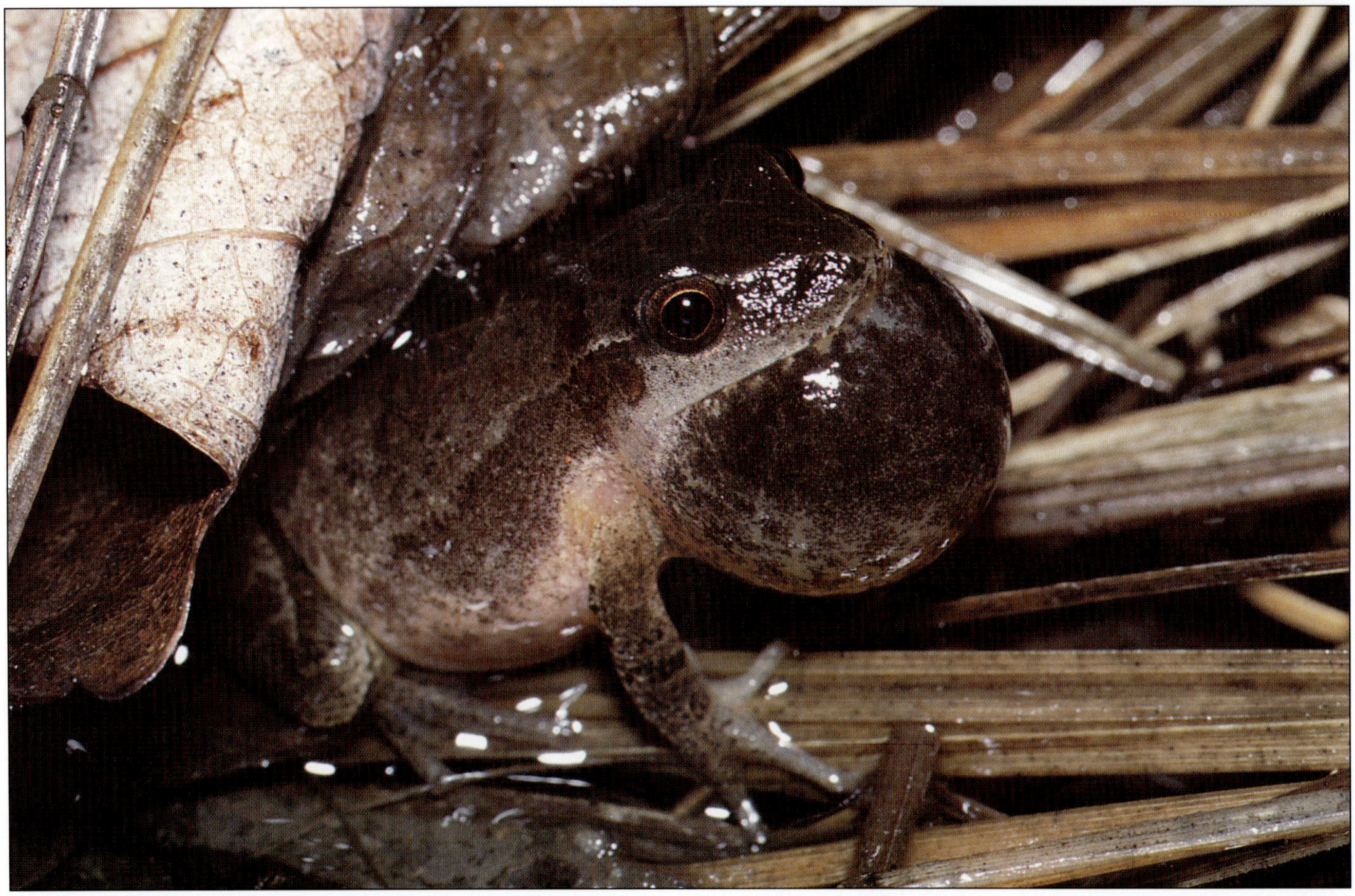

BELOW The loudest voice of the springtime marsh belongs to the spring peeper, a tiny tree frog whose shrill calls can be heard as much as a mile away.

insulation against cold water. But such boots are expensive, and for a one-time trip to the marsh, try this: Over jeans and thick wool socks, pull two heavy-duty garbage bags over each leg, then slip your feet inside an old pair of sneakers. Heavy rubber bands at the shins, knee and thighs will keep the bags in place. This cheap alternative is good for groups of children, although care must be taken to avoid ripping the plastic.

There is no special flashlight needed, although you may want to make a filter of red plastic to fit the front. Most mammals cannot see red light well, and a red beam may not disturb a raccoon, mink or muskrat that you come across.

The best season for such an excursion is spring. Then, the amphibian chorus will be in full voice, filling the night air with its calls. Amphibians lay eggs covered in a gelatinous layer that must stay wet in order to hatch, unlike the eggs of the more sophisticated reptiles, which have a water-tight shell. So even those frogs, toads and salamanders that spend most of their life on land must return to the water to breed, and the next generation will pass its first stage as gill-bearing tadpoles or larvae.

The salamanders come silently. In very early spring – even before the ice completely melts – the big mole salamanders, like the black and yellow spotted salamander, crawl out of their hibernation sites in the watery mud to breed. Their globular egg masses are laid on sunken branches or clumps of submerged grass by the females, then fertilized immediately by the attending males.

Frogs and toads advertise their presence, and it is their songs that give the nocturnal marsh its unique character. In the eastern U.S. and Canada, one of the first frogs to sing each year is the spring peeper, a tiny tree frog with a dark X mark on its back. The peeper's call is a loud, shrill *"reee-e-e-p"* which, in chorus, is audible more than a mile away. Finding the frog in a flashlight beam is hard, though, since the peepers nearby will fall silent. Turn off your flashlight and wait quietly for several minutes. When they begin calling again, try to pin one down by ear, then cover the front of the flashlight with your hand, allowing only a sliver of light to escape. Look carefully at the waterline, beneath overhanging vegetation, where the peeper males like to hide while singing.

Looking for amphibians, you are sure to find other nocturnal marsh residents. One is the six-spotted fishing spider, a large, hairy species that skates along on the surface tension of the water in much the same way as do smaller water striders seen by day. The fishing spider is a hunter, however, taking small fish, tadpoles and insects caught in its powerful fangs. In many marshes you may find leeches, undulating gracefully in mid-water. Despite their blood-sucking reputation, most feed on small invertebrates, frog eggs and the like, and pose no threat to humans.

A flashlight beam shining in the water for a long period of time will attract minute invertebrates, as a street lamp draws moths. These tiny creatures lure larger predators like diving beetles and backswimmers, which in turn may pull in small fish – a whole food chain, operating under the gaze of your light.

OPPOSITE TOP A six-spotted fishing spider skates along the surface tension of the water, ready to grab a tadpole minnow or insect that might swim beneath it.

BELOW A male American toad grabs a female in an embrace called amplexus; when she begins laying her eggs, he will fertilize them as they emerge.

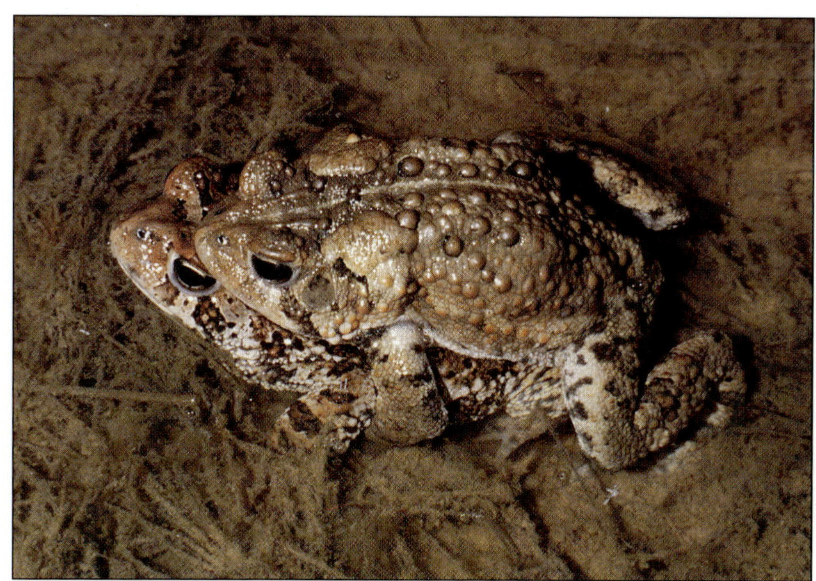

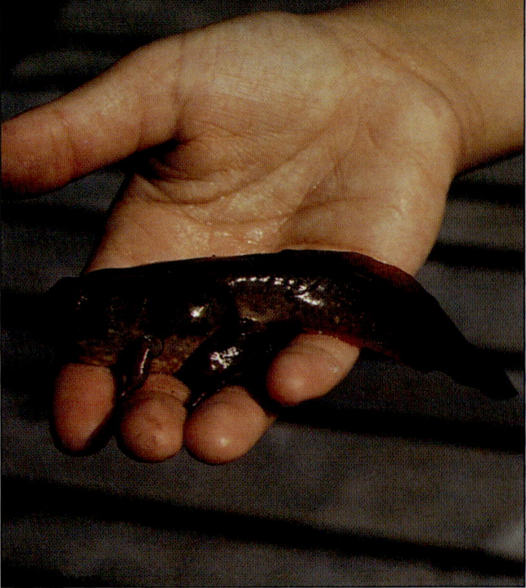

RIGHT Its legs growing and tail shrinking, this bullfrog tadpole is ready to be released, since its diet will be changing from vegetarian to carnivorous.

RAISING FROGS AND TADPOLES

RECOMMENDED EQUIPMENT
- Collecting bucket and plastic bags
- Small aquarium, filter and air pump

Just about every country child (and a lot of city kids, too) have had the thrill of watching a jar of frog eggs magically transform into wriggling tadpoles, and later begin to sprout legs for the metamorphosis into adult frogs. The process is endlessly fascinating, and a great way to inaugurate spring each year.

Finding amphibian eggs is usually no problem; almost any marsh, swamp and pond will have them in early spring, although the species will vary with the habitat. Frogs usually lay their eggs in compact masses or sheets, while American toads lay long, spiraling ropes of eggs that may stretch 25 feet or more. Handle the egg mass gently, without ripping it, which might allow fungi and bacteria to reach the eggs. Reject any that contain eggs that are white or fuzzy – these are infected with fungi, which may spread to the rest. (Also avoid collecting the large, globular egg masses of mole salamanders, since the salamander larvae are predaceous, and are very difficult to keep in captivity.)

Exercise restraint, taking only one or two small masses. Transport them home in a plastic bag of water, then transfer them to a small aquarium; if you fill the tank with tap water, use an antichlorine chemical or allow the water to stand for several days before getting the eggs. A small undergravel filter and aeration unit, while not essential, will ensure good water quality.

In a warm house, the eggs will develop quickly – so quickly, in fact, that one can see the growth on an almost hourly basis, as the cells split and specialize. Soon, a groove forms along the egg, which will later fold over into a tube, the crude beginnings of the frog's spinal column. But when the tadpole hatches, it will look nothing like a frog – or even what most people think a tadpole looks like. It will have feathery gills and a mouth, but no real eyes, and its swimming ability will be poor.

Once all the tadpoles have hatched (it may take a day or two) remove the empty egg mass. Feed the tadpoles finely chopped lettuce, adding tiny bits of mashed, raw meat when the tads are several weeks old. Be sure not to feed so much that the water fouls, and change it with dechlorinated water of the same temperature once or twice a week.

It is possible to raise tadpoles to adulthood, but as their diet changes from vegetable matter to meat it becomes increasingly difficult to feed them. It is better to release them once their leg growth becomes pronounced and the shape of the mouth begins to change. Take them back to their home pond and float their transport bag for 15 minutes to equalize the temperature. Thanks to the warm home and abundant food, they should be quite a bit larger than their cousins that stayed behind.

BELOW Less than a day old, the eggs of a wood frog clearly show how the cells are dividing and specializing to form the embryo.

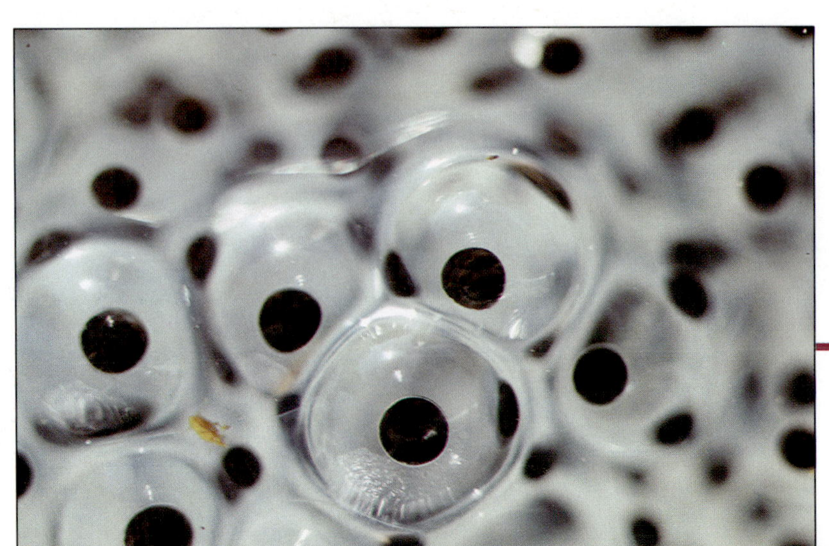

BUILDING A TURTLE PLATFORM

On a warm, bright day, there's nothing a turtle enjoys more than hauling itself out of the water and sunning on a fallen log. But good sunning locations aren't always available – or they may be too far away or hidden to provide good viewing for you.

There are two solutions. Placing large logs along stream and lake shores will provide natural sunning spots, but a better idea is a custom-built platform.

The design is fairly simple. The base should be made of three 8-foot lengths of cedar log, about 8 inches in diameter. To the base, nail 4-foot lengths of 2-by-6 pine board, leaving a quarter-inch gap between the boards. Do not use pressure-treated lumber, since the copper-based preservative is toxic when wet. Refer to the appendix for plans. The finished platform fills the two main requirements that basking turtles have – a flat haul-out area, and a low profile that allows the turtles to easily crawl out of the water. Anchor the platform in a sunny spot, at least 15 feet from shore for predator protection. Use chain and concrete blocks for anchors, and secure the platform at opposite corners to keep it from swinging in the wind.

Ducks and geese will also use the platforms for resting and preening, especially since they are essentially predator free. Larger, modified platforms, heaped with marsh vegetation, have been used as nesting platforms for common loons, whose lakeside nests are often swamped by fluctuating water levels and power boat wakes.

BELOW Most freshwater turtles need a place to climb out of the water and bask in the sun. Natural logs work, but a turtle platform can afford greater protection from predators.

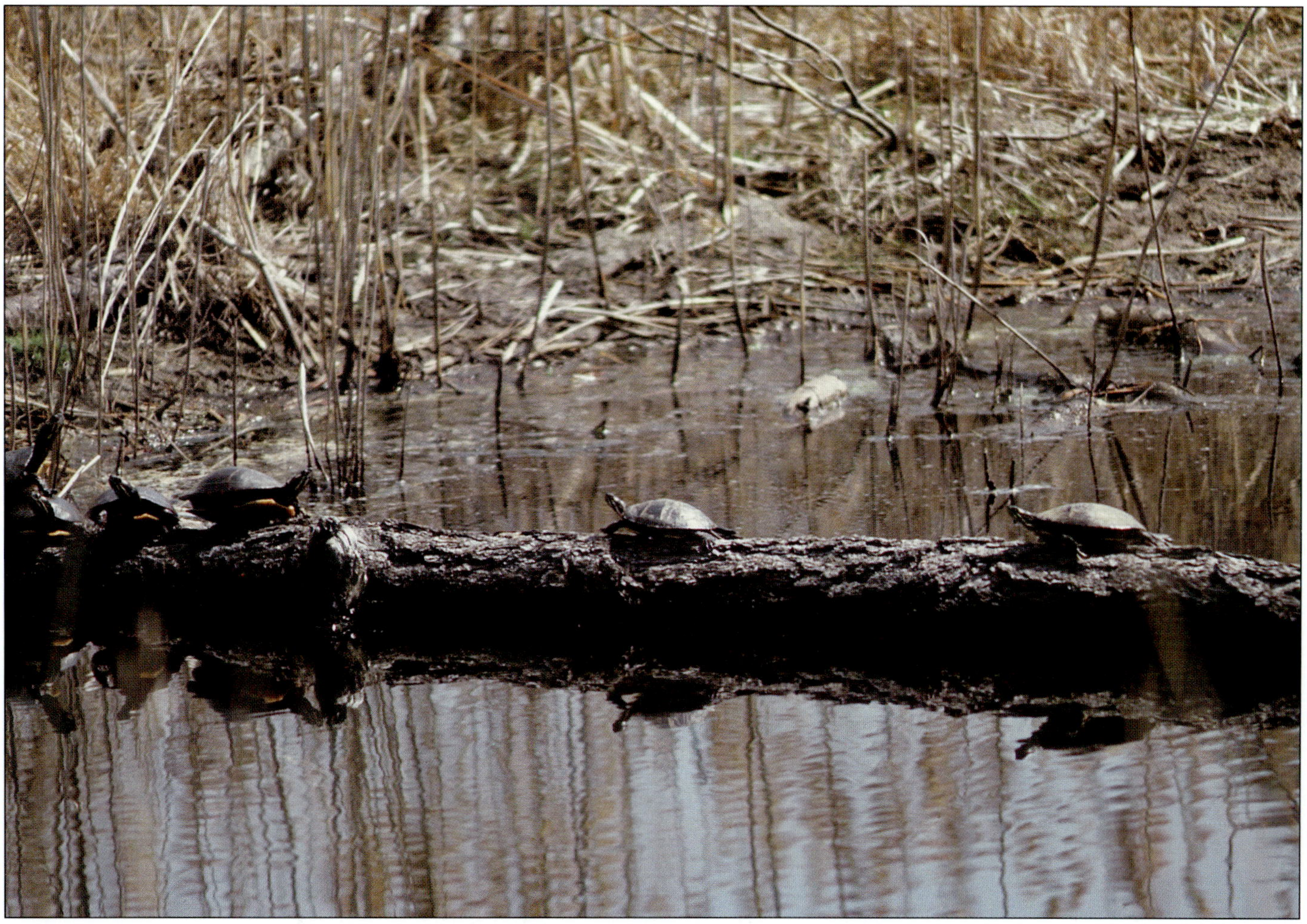

FINDING AND OBSERVING SNAKES

RECOMMENDED EQUIPMENT
- Binoculars (optional)

Snakes must be the least-loved animals in the world, a bias due largely to fear and ignorance. In truth, snakes are beautiful, fascinating animals, and although a few varieties are poisonous, none will attack without provocation.

Snakes are not just legless lizards, as many people think, although they evolved from an ancestral lizard stock about 100 million years ago. Instead of legs, they move with a combination of motions: S-curves, in which the snake's body pushes against the outside edge of the curve, and a caterpillar-like movement of the belly scales that allows the snake to move in a straight line over rough surfaces. Snake have no ears, and so are deaf to most air-borne vibration, but they are very sensitive to vibration transmitted through the ground.

Although they have nostrils, snakes do not smell in the sense we are familiar with. Rather, they flick out their tongue, picking up odor particles from the air and placing them in a specialized sensing organ in the roof of the mouth. It is not too far from the truth, then, to say that a snake is "tasting" the air with its tongue. Contrary to folk beliefs, no snake can sting with its tongue – or, for that matter, with its tail.

Because snakes can sense approaching footsteps, observing them in the wild takes stealth and patience, as well as a knowledge of snake habits. Being cold-blooded, snakes regulate their body temperature by moving back and forth between sun and shade. On a cool day, or in early spring and late fall, look for snakes sunning themselves on rock ledges and logs in the sunshine. Conversely, on hot days it is best to go afield early, since the snakes will retreat to hidden nooks when the temperature starts to rise. Macadam roads, which retain heat from the day and radiate it after the sun goes down, are a magnet for snakes, especially in desert regions where the temperature falls quickly after dark.

Searching the proper habitat will also increase your chances of finding snakes. Poke carefully around rocky outcroppings (being very careful where you place your hands and feet, if venomous species may be present), brushpiles and log heaps, stone walls and along the edge of ponds, creeks and rivers. Train your eyes to separate the smooth curves of the snake's body from the jumble of angular branches, leaves and grass that form the background. Once you find a snake, particularly one that is basking, you may be able to locate it

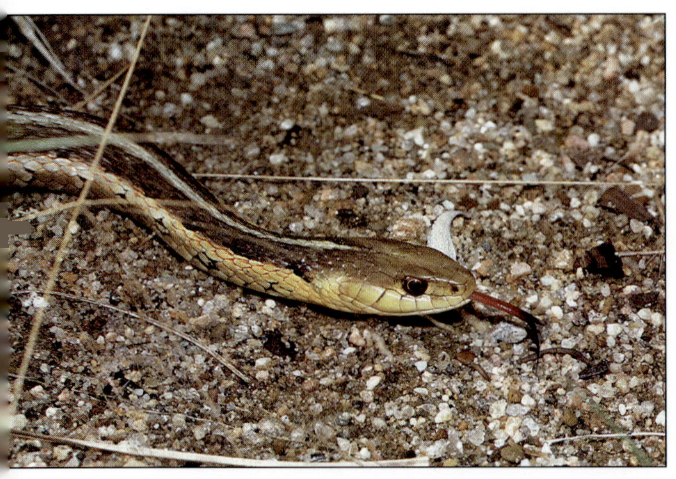

BELOW Far from being a poisonous stinger, a snake's tongue is a harmless tool, picking up odor molecules and transferring them to a sensory organ in the roof of the mouth. This is an eastern garter snake.

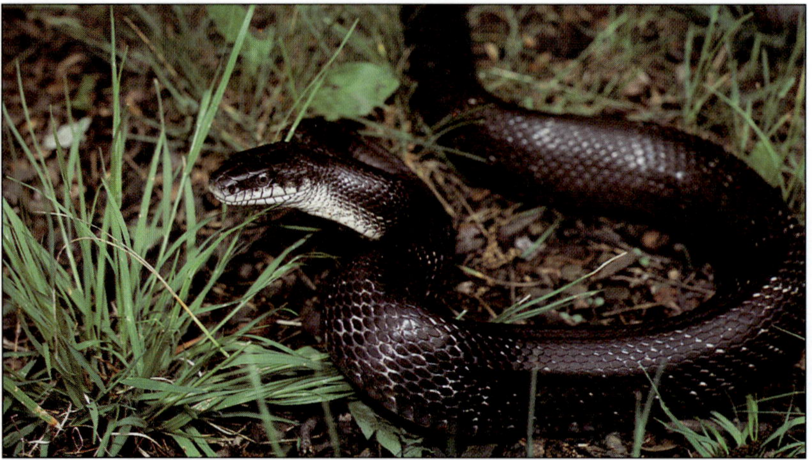

BELOW RIGHT Even nonpoisonous snakes will bite if provoked. This black rat snake has drawn itself up in a tight S-coil, and is buzzing its tail in the leaves as a warning.

again and again in the same spot, if you do not disturb it with your approach.

Patience is also required once you find a snake to watch, because these reptiles live life at a very slow pace. Especially if it has fed recently, a snake may do absolutely nothing for hours on end except bask in the sun and digest the lump in its middle. Sometimes, though, you stumble across a snake engaged in an engrossing activity. If you locate a snake whose eyes are clouded, check again in a day or two, for it is preparing to shed; the eyes will clear several hours before shedding, but the skin will still appear dull and lusterless. The snake will begin the process by rubbing its snout against a rock or branch, until the outer layer of skin begins to peel away. It keeps rubbing, and the grayish, translucent skin pulls off in one piece, inside out, like a long tube sock. Every scale, including the ocular scale that covers the snake's lidless eye, comes off intact – on many shed skins, you can even see a hint of the color pattern, allowing identification even if you did not see the snake itself.

Feeding is equally interesting. Snake cannot chew their prey, which is swallowed in one piece, often alive, although some constrictors and most venomous snakes kill before eating. The lower jaws unhinge from the skull and from each other, allowing the snake's mouth to stretch to fantastic proportions as it engulfs its prey. Do not disturb a snake that has eaten recently, since it may regurgitate its food. Digestion can take several days, and the snake may feed only once a week in cool weather.

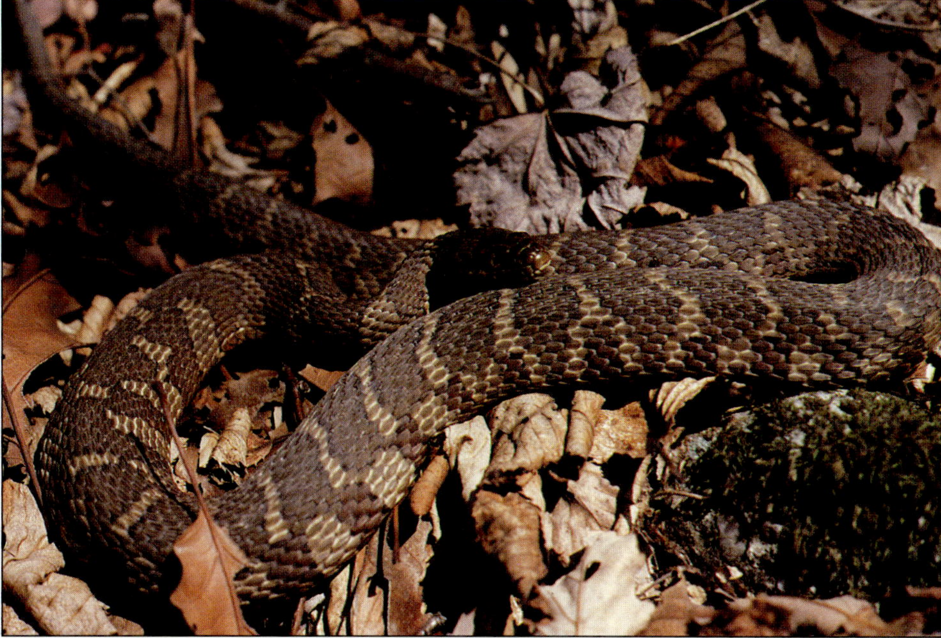

ABOVE Most of a snake's life is spent doing little or nothing. This northern water snake (a common, harmless species), is basking in the sun on a chilly spring day, trying to raise its body temperature.

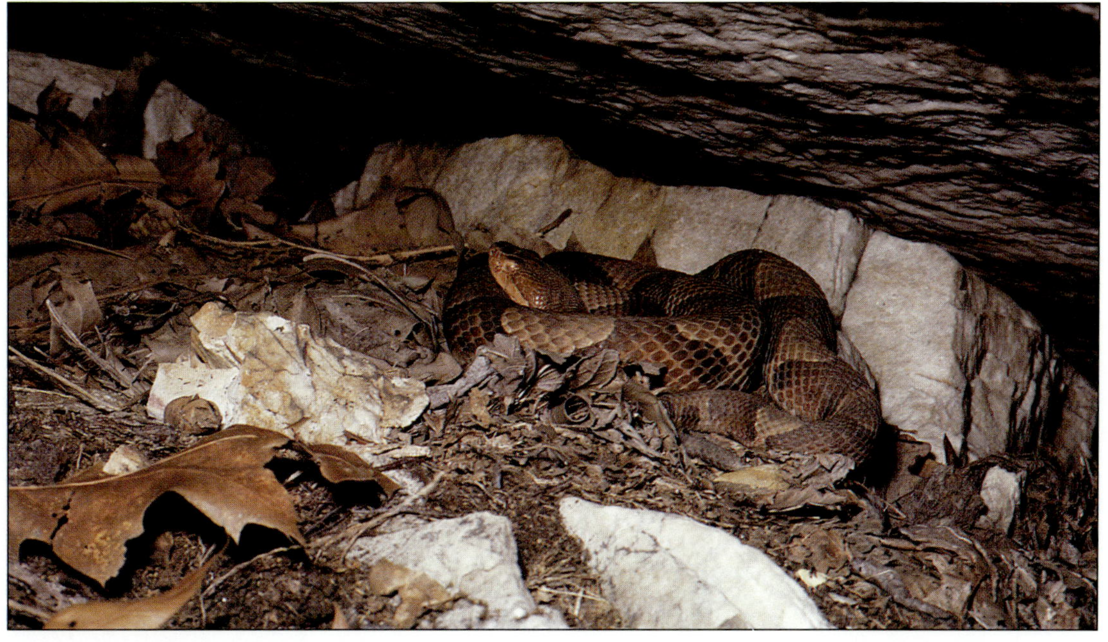

LEFT Hidden from the hot midday sun, a northern copperhead rests beneath a rocky ledge. Poisonous but mild-tempered, the copperhead is found from southern New England to Texas.

ATTRACTING AND STUDYING BATS

RECOMMENDED EQUIPMENT

- "Bat houses"

Like snakes, bats are another animal that have suffered from an ill-deserved bad reputation. Far from being verminous, blood-sucking monsters, they are clean, highly adapted insect-eaters that pose no more threat to humans than any other small mammal.

More and more people apparently agree, as evidenced by the rising sales of commercially made "bat houses," which attract colonies of breeding females. The helping hand comes not a moment too soon, for bat populations are dropping drastically in many areas, as bats suffer from habitat loss and the contamination of their food supply by insecticides.

Bats are not mice with wings; they are insectivores, more closely related to shrews and moles than to rodents. They are the only mammals capable of true flight ("flying" squirrels can only glide), thanks to their greatly elongated foreleg and digit bones, covered by a thin webbing of skin. Hunting after dark, they emit a rapid series of chirps at ultrahigh frequencies, which bounce off their prey and echo back, relaying to the bat the insect's size, shape, direction and speed. The insect is caught

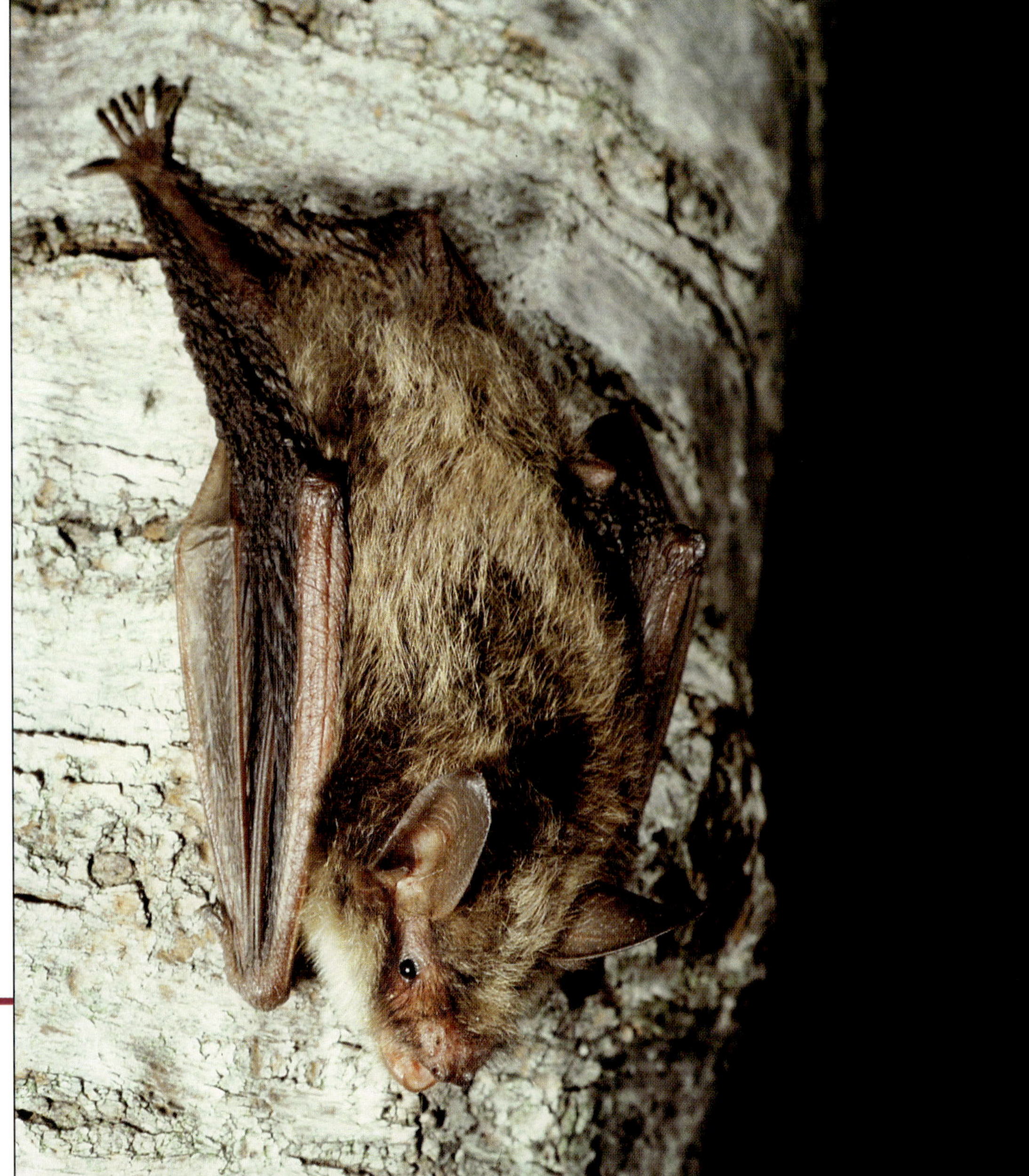

RIGHT Objects of fear and superstition, bats (like this little brown bat) are clean, harmless and fascinating animals that do not deserve their bad reputation.

while the bat is on the wing, usually in the membrane between the legs and tail, or in a cupped wing, then transferred to the mouth and eaten.

There are about 38 species of bats in the U.S. and Canada, falling into several large groups. The solitary, heavily furred tree bats are the most northerly, with two species found as far north as the arctic rim of Hudson Bay. In the Southwest, free-tailed bats congregate in caves, often by the millions. But over most of North America, the most common backyard bat is the little brown bat, or little brown myotis, whose fluttering flights are so much a part of the summer evening.

Little brown bats hibernate in caves, tunnels, mine shafts and other sheltered areas with constant temperature and high humidity. In summer, though, the males are solitary, while the females form nursery colonies in attics, barn eaves and other places where the temperature is high. Each female ordinarily has one young, which may be carried along, clinging to its mother's fur for the first few days, but which stays roosting in the colony later, when it becomes heavier. The young bats take to the air when about a month old, but the colony will continue to use the roost until they depart for the winter.

A bat colony in the walls or attic of a house can cause a serious odor and annoyance problem, as well as increasing the chance of bats getting into the living quarters of the home. A properly placed bat box may lure them away, especially if any hole wider than ¼ inch is plugged before they return in the spring. The box is built along the same lines as a birdhouse, but with an entrance slit on the bottom rather than a front hole. Inside, a partition that comes almost to the floor divides the box into two compartments for maximum use. Plans for a bat box appear in the appendix of this book.

The box can be mounted to the side of a building or a tree trunk, as long as it will be exposed to direct sun to keep the temperatures inside at roughly 90 degrees; some people paint the roof and upper third black to help it absorb heat. The wood used for the inside and partition should be rough, to give the bats good footing.

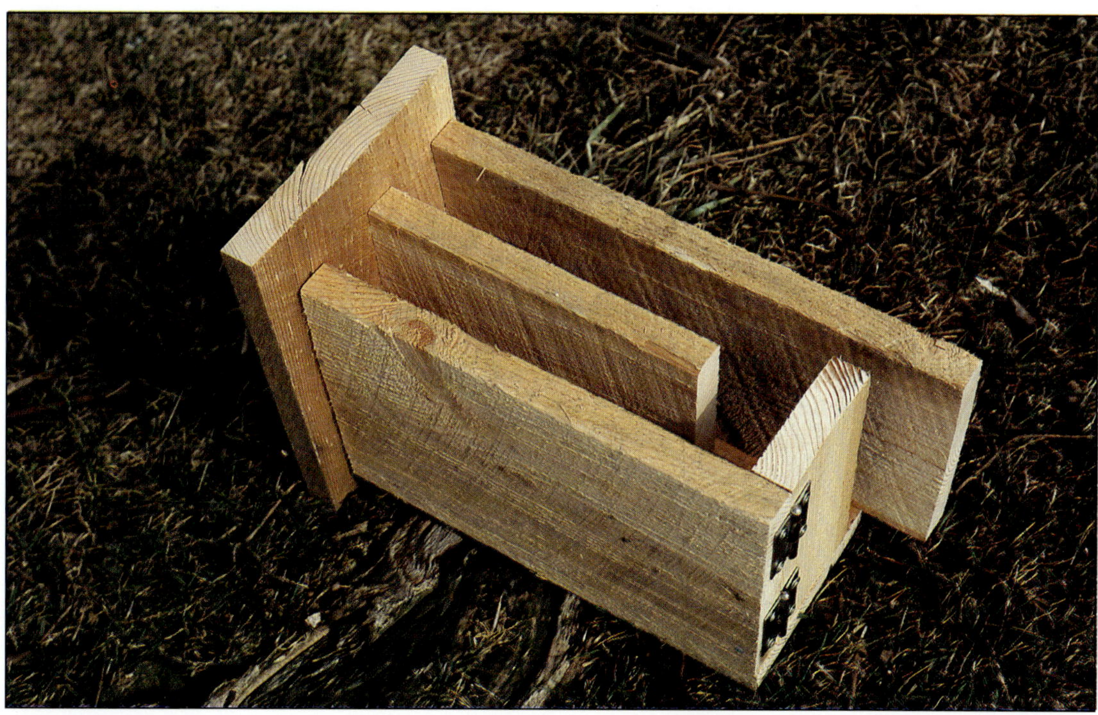

LEFT A bat house, with the side removed to show the interior partition. Note the hinged floor, and the use of rough-finished lumber, which gives the bats better footing.

RIGHT A blanket of fresh snow makes the winter woods seem even more lifeless than usual, but there are many animals and plants that continue their lives despite the cold.

EXPLORING THE WINTER WOODS

RECOMMENDED EQUIPMENT
- Binoculars
- Hand lens

At first glance, a forest blanketed in thick winter snow seems to be lifeless. Gone are the flickering leaves and wildflowers of summer, the constant hum of flying insects and the songs of breeding birds. The silence can be oppressive.

To a naturalist's eyes, of course, the winter woods are very much alive, although at a slower pace than the rush of mid-summer. All the reptiles and amphibians, along with a few of the mammals, are hibernating, while a majority of the song-birds have migrated south for the winter. Those birds that remain, however, are the most obvious residents of the forest.

In the mixed deciduous woods of the Northeast, the most endearing winter bird is the black-capped chickadee, also found across the rest of the northern U.S. and southern Canada. The chickadee is an irrepressible mite, barely 5 inches long and weighing less than an ounce, but with a curiosity as big as all outdoors. Its *chick-a-dee-dee-dee* calls are a signature sound of the winter forest, announcing the passage of a flock. Interestingly, the flock will probably contain a mix of other species, usually titmice, nuthatches and wood-peckers. Because each forages for dormant insects in a different way they do not compete, and the larger group offers better protection from predators.

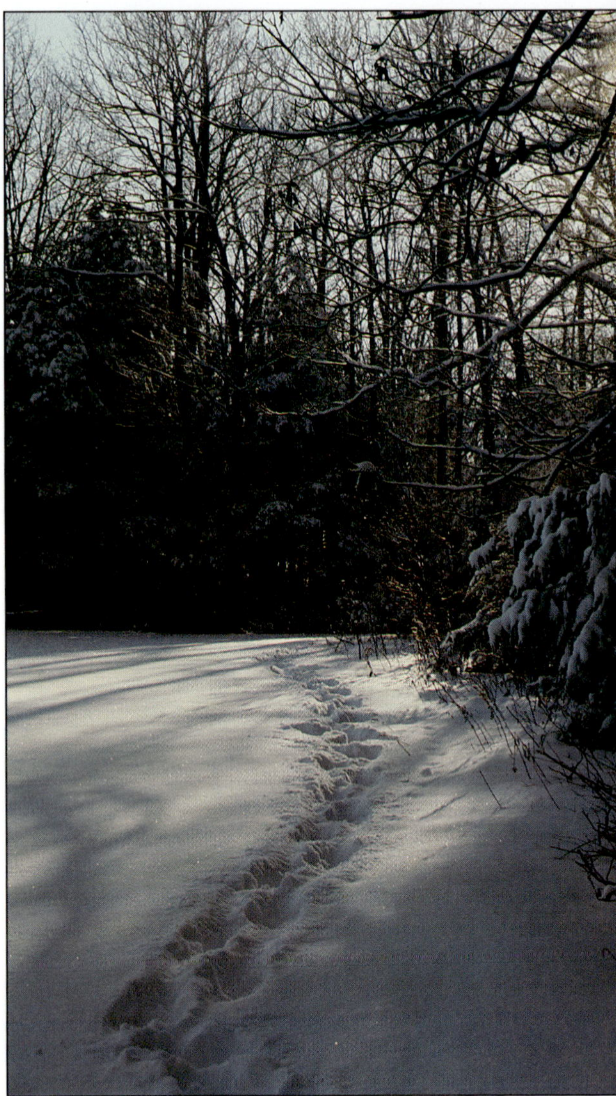

BELOW Christmas fern is one of several evergreen ferns that can be found through the winter.

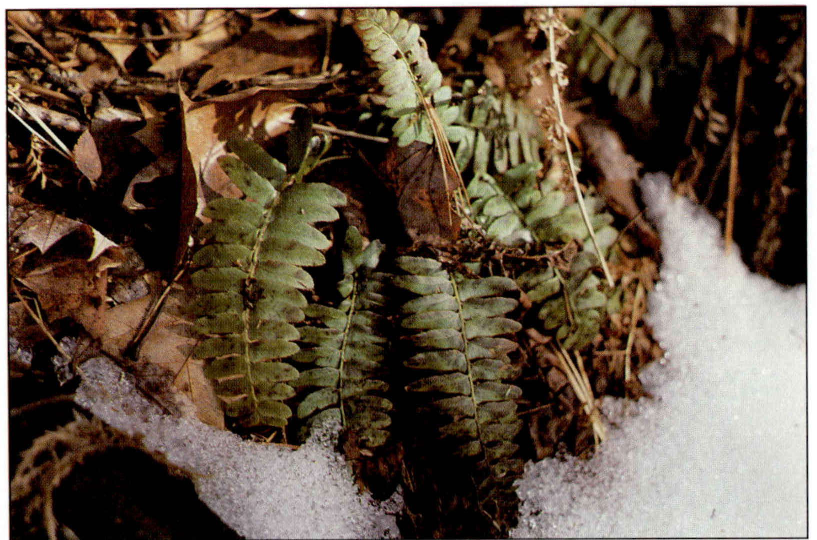

Even smaller than the chickadee are the kinglets, both golden- and ruby-crowned species, just 4 inches long. The kinglets probably represent the smallest size that a warm-blooded animal can have and still survive the frigid weather. The key is sur-face area; the smaller an animal becomes, the more surface area (which loses body heat) it has in relation to body mass (which generates heat). In order to keep up with the demands of its racing metabolism and constant heat loss, the kinglet – like all songbirds – must eat enormous quantities of seeds and insects in order to survive.

Larger animals have the advantage of greater mass to cushion them from the cold. Generally speaking, northern animals are bigger than southern individuals of the same species, which explains why white-tailed deer from the Maine woods may weigh 250 pounds, compared to the dog-sized Key deer of south Florida. Members of the deer family including moose, elk and caribou, are insulated further from the cold by specially adapted hair that functions on the principle of a thermos bottle. A white-tail's hair, for instance, is hollow, so not only does the pelt trap air between the hairs, each hair has its own chamber to add to the insulation. A deer can bed down in the snow during the day, yet melt almost none of it beneath its body.

The insects that filled the summer forest have all dropped into dormancy for the winter. Many overwinter as eggs that will hatch in the spring; others as larvae or pupae. Peel away a section of bark from a dead tree, and you'll find cocoons and chrysalises, silk-covered egg masses, adult spiders tucked inside protective webs, dormant beetles and other arthropods. It is this hidden storehouse of insects that the wintering birds are seeking, and they will be sure to find what you have uncovered.

Some insects are more adaptable to the cold than others. The seemingly delicate mourning cloak butterfly is a common sight on mild winter days, flying slowly through among the trees. The butterfly's wings are a dark maroon color with yellow edges; when it emerges from beneath bark slabs, it orients its open wings to the sun, which warms the dark surface and brings the butterfly's body temperature up high enough to allow flight.

Also on mild days, the snow may seem dirty, as though someone had spilled a jar of black pepper across it. Look more closely and you'll see that each fleck is alive – and capable of remarkably long jumps. They are springtails, also known as snow fleas, minute scavengers that occur by the millions in forest leaf litter.

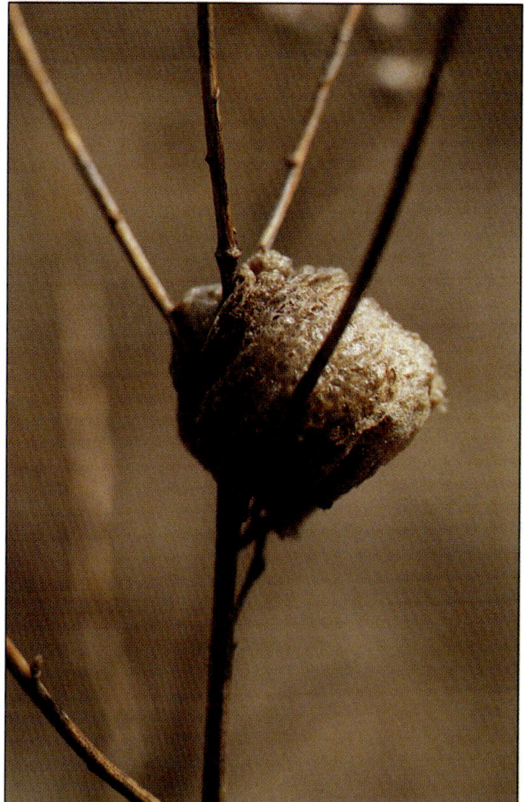

LEFT Along weedy woodland edges, watch for the globular egg masses of praying mantids – but do not take them indoors, where the sudden warmth will trigger the hundreds of eggs inside to hatch.

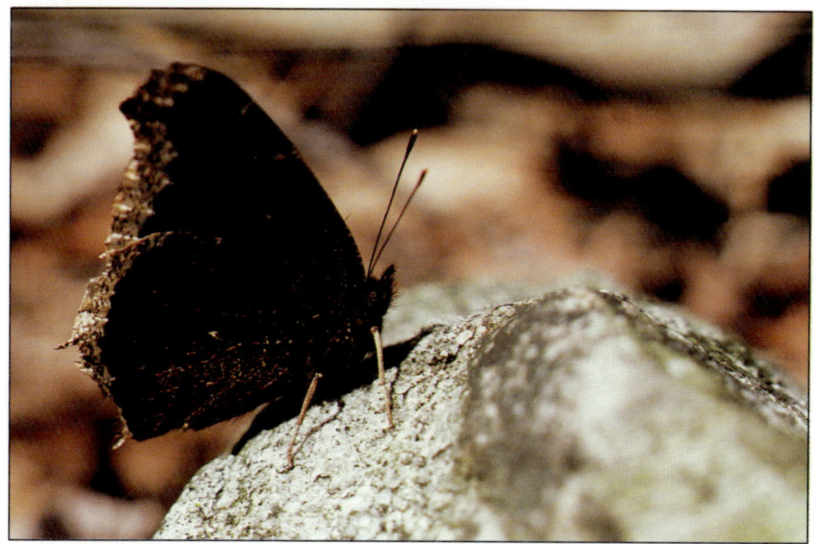

BELOW On mild winter days, the mourning cloak butterfly emerges from dormancy; its dark wings absorb solar heat better than the light-colored wings of summer species.

RIGHT Tracks lead away from an oak, showing where a gray squirrel bounded off to another tree.

TRACKING ANIMALS IN SNOW OR DIRT

Tracking animals takes no special equipment, but it does call for a good imagination. An experienced tracker, reading the mute prints, can recreate what the animal was doing, feeling – perhaps even what it was thinking. Tracking is a way to get inside the head of a wild animal.

The first step is identifying the tracks, of course. By far the best guide available is *A Field Guide to Animal Tracks* by Olaus J. Murie, number 9 in the Peterson Field Guide series. In exhaustive detail, the book covers the tracks and signs left by all of North America's mammals, as well as birds, reptiles and amphibians, and even insects.

The best tracking conditions come after a wet snow. The ideal depth is about two or three inches – deep enough to cover the leaves and grass, but not so deep that the walls of the track fall in on themselves. Wait until a night has passed before going afield, to give the animals a chance to leave their mark, then go out early in the morning, before the sun begins to melt the snow and disfigures the tracks.

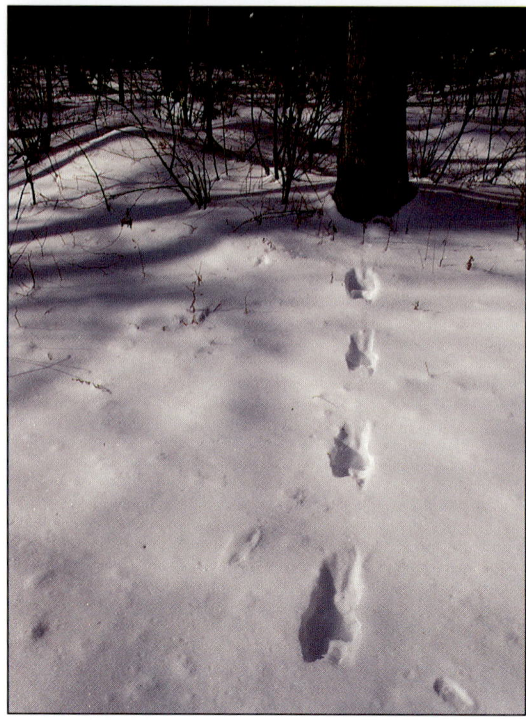

BELOW Fresh, wet snow is the best medium for tracking. Go out early in the morning, before the sun has a chance to blur the crisp tracks; these were left by a herd of white-tailed deer.

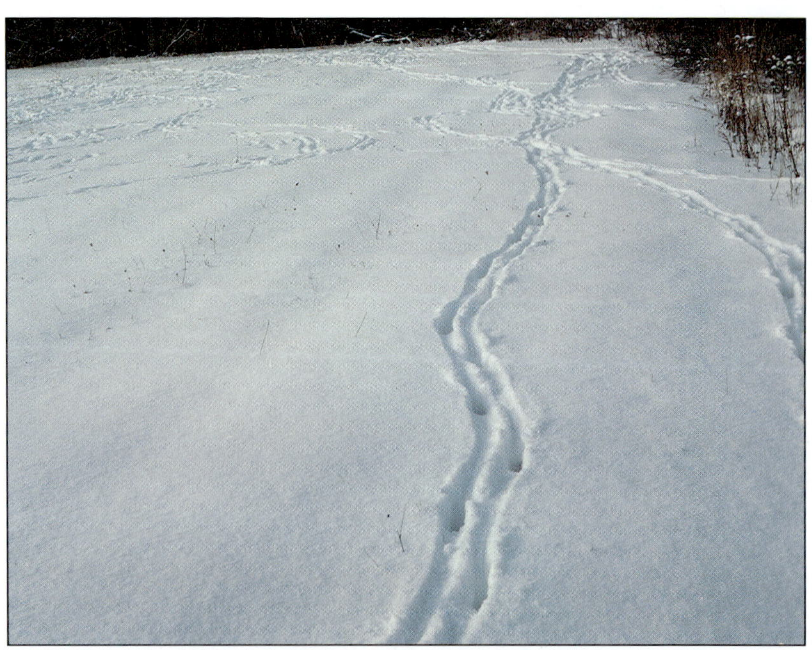

Walk alongside a trail – never on the tracks. Let each print tell its own story – a deer track with splayed hooves and skid marks indicates a running animal, for instance. But read the trail as a whole, too. Be aware of direction, pace, the distance between tracks. Look ahead. Was the deer heading for a field to feed, or for thick conifers to bed down? If a coyote trail shows long, loping strides, a sudden stop and then small steps, circle ahead – you may find the tracks of the jackrabbit the coyote was stalking.

Although tracking is easiest in snow, an observant naturalist can follow a trail over many different surfaces. A running deer or feeding turkey will kick up leaves that appear darker than those of the forest floor, while an animal passing through a dewy lawn or field will disturb the dewdrops and leave a trail. Mud is almost as good as snow, especially if the animal is following a riverbed, traveling through muddy soil for long distances. In fact, waterways are among the most rewarding places to look for tracks, since so many animals are drawn to them. Probably the most common prints

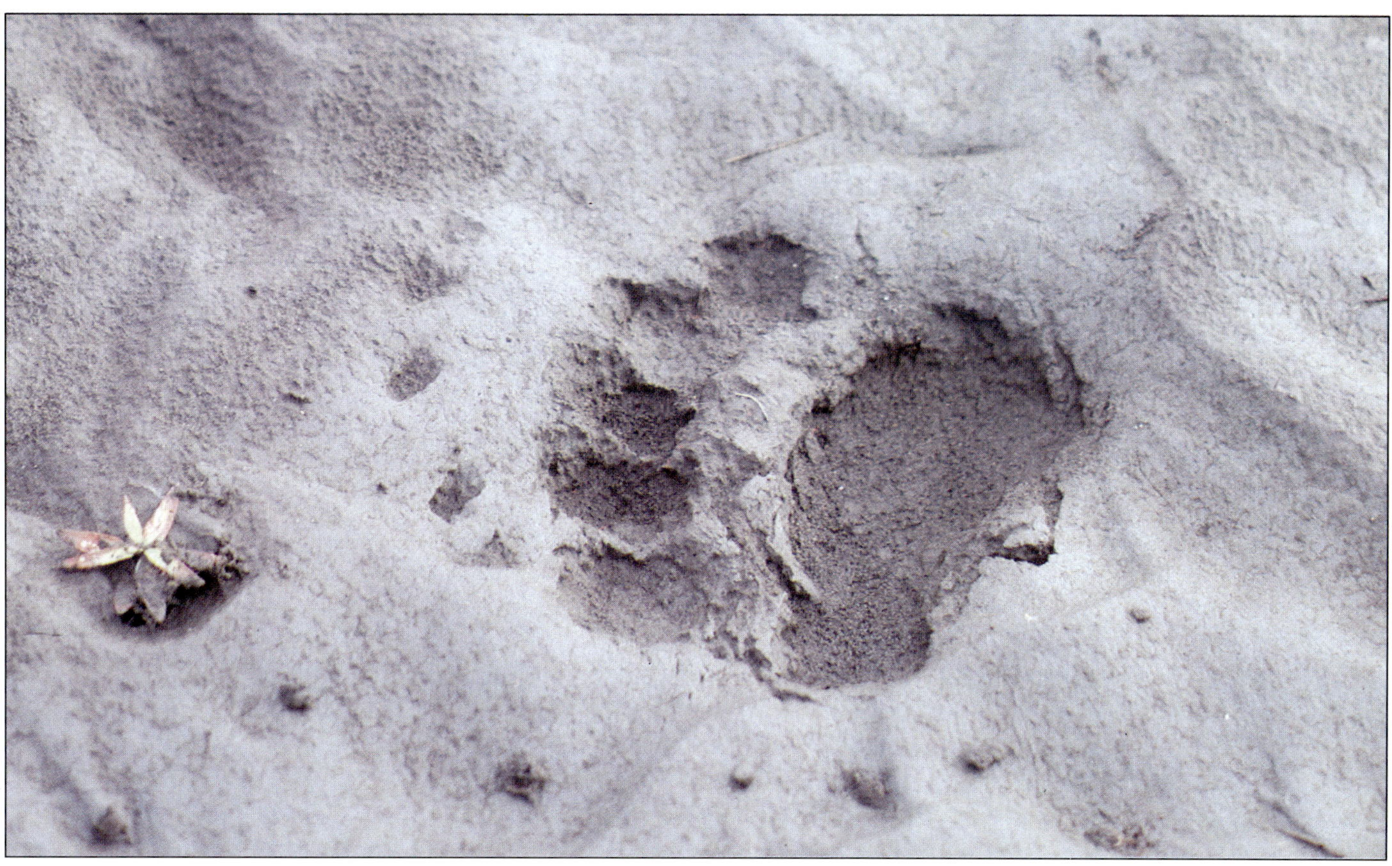

will be the handlike tracks of the raccoon, wandering in and out of the water, showing the places the 'coon explored for food. You may find the remains of its meal as you follow the trail – the claws of a crayfish, bluegills scales or the collapsed shells of turtle eggs that it dug out of their underground nest.

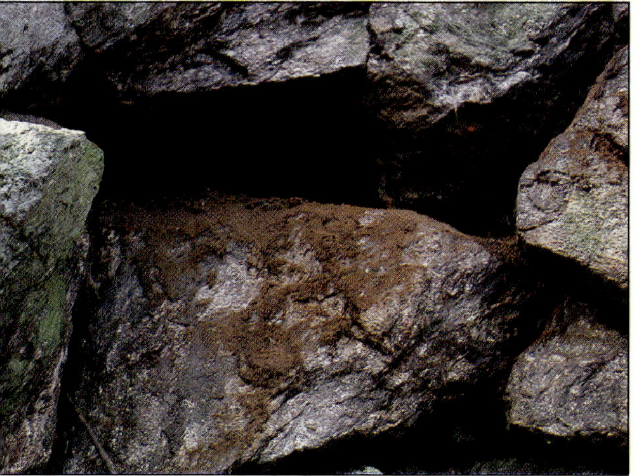

Dust is an excellent tracking surface in the summer, although it is best to be up and around first thing in the morning, before the breeze obliterates the tracks. A country dirt road will reveal a wealth of tracks, often in exquisite detail. The paw prints of a red fox will show the fine hair marks between the pads; the tracks of a ring-necked pheasant, meandering out of nearby fields, may even indicate the corrugation on the foot surface itself.

Most of the tracks you will find will be invertebrate, however. Many will not be identifiable, but some groups of insects leave characteristic signs. Beetles, for instance, usually make a furrow in the dust, stitched with an endless series of tiny, comma-shaped footprints. Grasshopper and cricket trails will be broken from short hops. If the previous night was damp, the most common trails may be those of earthworms, long, sinuous tracks with silver where the worm's slime trail has dried.

ABOVE A track is a fleeting record of an animal's passage – in this case, a grizzly bear that ambled down a muddy riverbed in central Alaska.

LEFT Be alert for signs other than tracks; this accumulation of dropping shows that porcupines are using the cave as a winter den.

MAKING PLASTER CASTS OF TRACKS

RECOMMENDED EQUIPMENT

- Plaster of Paris mix
- Mixing jar
- Flask of water
- Atomizer
- One-inch wide strips of heavy paper and paper clips (optional)

Tracks are ephemeral – here one day, gone the next with the changing fortunes of wind, rain and snow. But they need not be lost completely. Plaster casts are a terrific way to make a permanent record of the tracks you find.

The procedure is simple. Choosing the print is the critical step; dirt and mud make the best casts, although it is possible to make a serviceable cast in snow if the plaster mix is very cold, and if you spray the track with water from an atomizer to form an icy coating in the print. In mud, wet sand or dirt, pick the clearest print, free from pebbles or debris, and choose one that has crisply defined edges.

Mix the plaster in a wide-mouthed jar; plastic margarine containers also work well. Add water to plaster, rather than the other way around, mixing it quickly to a slurry. Judging the right consistency takes practice and experience, but as a rule of thumb, when the mix "slows" and becomes as thick as melted ice cream, it is ready.

In most circumstances all you need to do is pour the plaster slowly into the tracking, making sure that no air bubbles are trapped along the bottom. Fill the track, then puddle the plaster over the edge to form a small mound. For a neater cast, take a 1-inch-wide strip of heavy paper, long enough to circle the track. Paper-clip the ends together and push it gently into the ground around the print, forming a dam for the plaster.

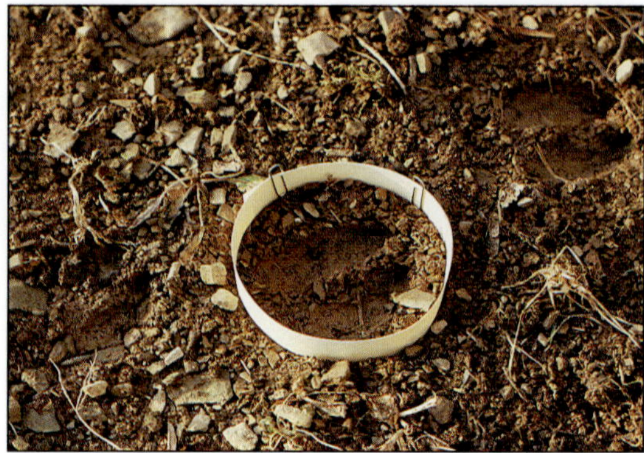

TOP RIGHT For a neater cast, make a collar of stiff paper and push it gently into the soil around the track.

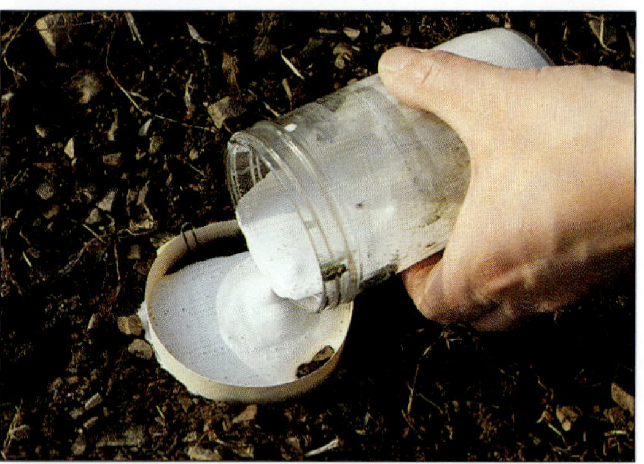

MIDDLE RIGHT While pouring the plaster into the track, be careful not to trap large air bubbles in the print.

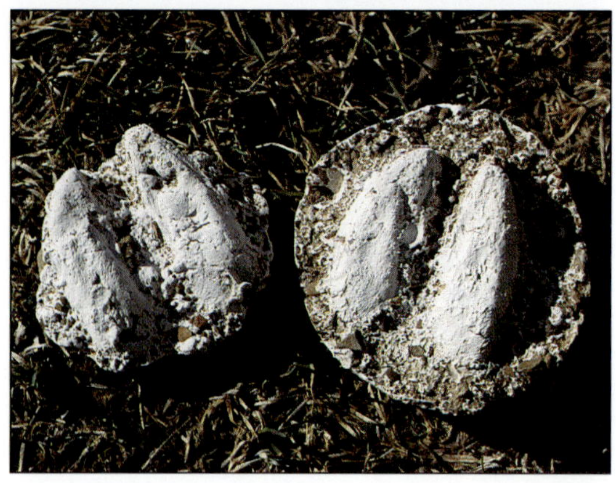

BOTTOM RIGHT After allowing the plaster to set thoroughly, dig up the cast and wash away the dirt. The cast on the left was made without a paper collar, simply by puddling paster into the track.

Allow the cast to harden thoroughly, bearing in mind that the top surface will harden more rapidly than the lower. It is better to let the cast set too long than not long enough – nothing is worse than removing a partially set cast, and having it fragment into useless pieces. When it is completely dry, do not pull it out of the ground. Instead, dig up the cast carefully, then wash away any clinging soil. Record the species, date and place in ink on the upper surface.

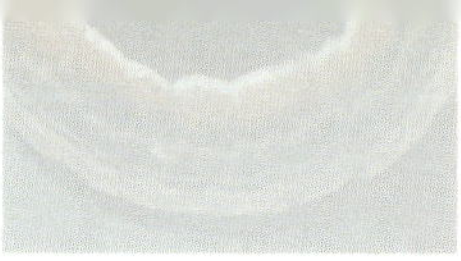

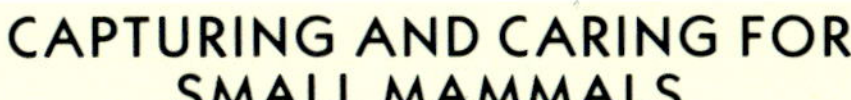

CAPTURING AND CARING FOR SMALL MAMMALS

RECOMMENDED EQUIPMENT
- Live-catch traps
- Aquaria and tight-fitting lids
- Light-weight leather gloves

While it is usually better to watch free, undisturbed animals to learn their behavior and life history, some kinds of wildlife are almost impossible to observe in the wild because they are so small or secretive. That is the case with most of the small mammals – mice, shrews, voles and their relatives. A majority of what we know about them comes from captive study.

Fortunately, small mammals are easy to capture and keep. The best traps to use are metal variations of the classic box-trap, which hold the animal harmlessly; Havahart, Sherman and other brands, in the smallest sizes, are preferred. For rodents, the best bait is a mixture of peanut butter, oatmeal and bacon fat, smeared on the bait pan. This mix also works for shrews, as will raw meat.

Small mammals generally follow regular pathways, marked by tunnels through the grass. Clear an opening for the trap, which should be set with its open ends aligned on the runway (in such circumstances, it may not even be necessary to use bait). Other good trapping sites include rock piles, along fallen logs, beside streams and ponds. Small mammals are highly habitat-specific – the yellow-nosed vole of eastern Canada, New England and the Appalachians is found in moist, mixed

BELOW Flying squirrels are excellent candidates for study, since they are tame and common. A live trap set on a tray feeder at a woodland bird feeding station will often catch them, since flying squirrels frequently visit feeders at night.

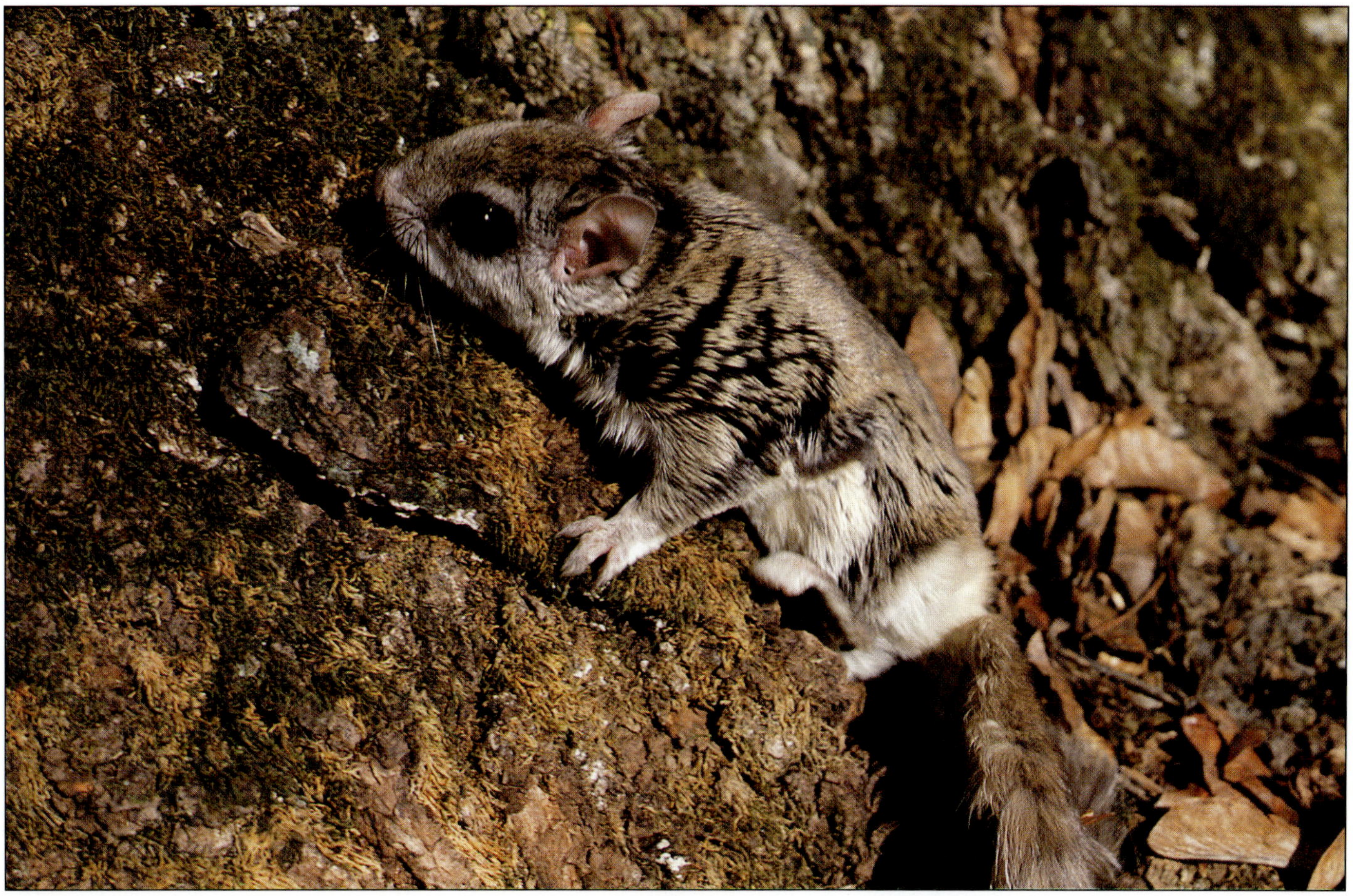

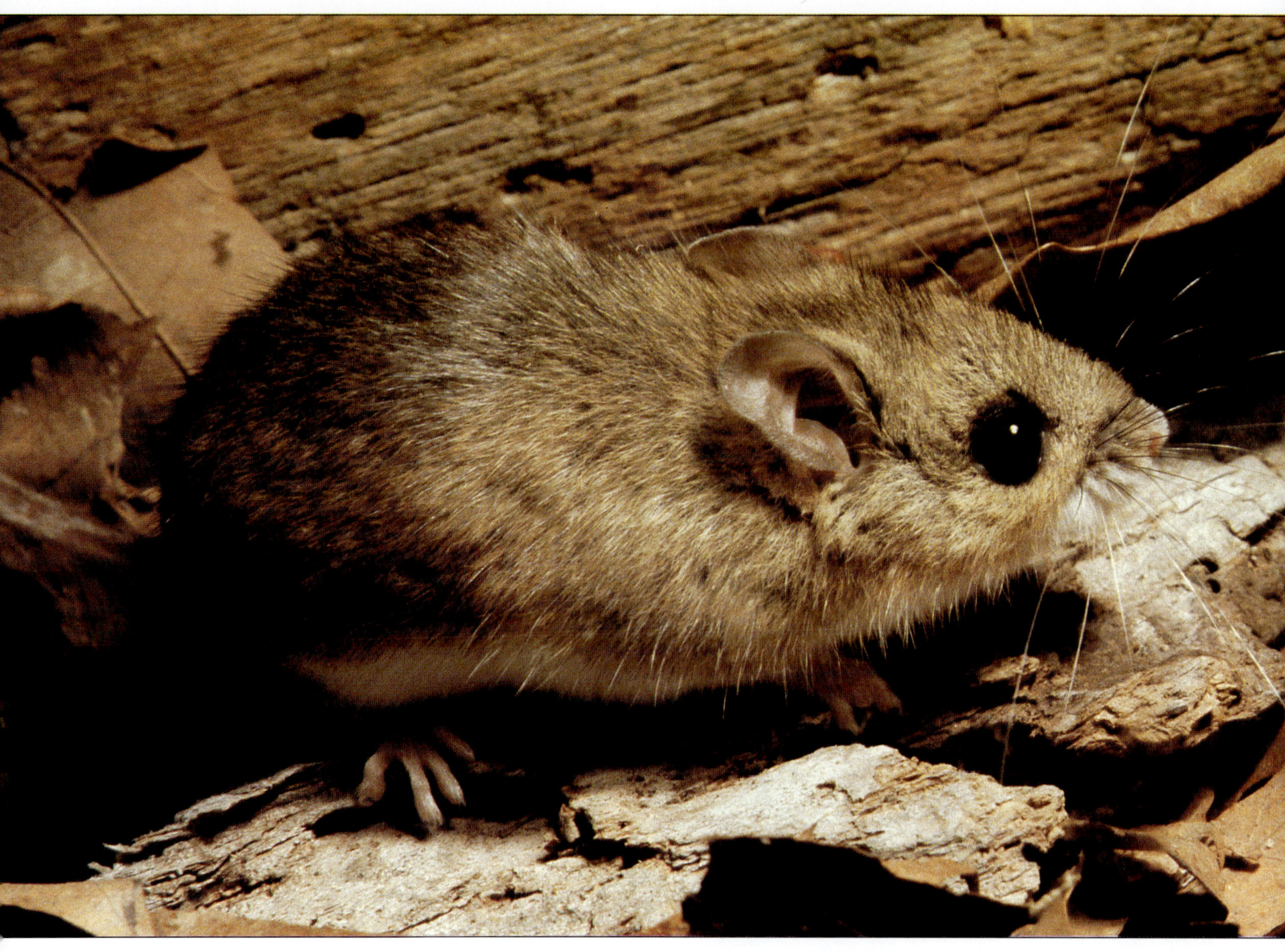

ABOVE The deer mouse is one of the most common small mammals in North America, and adapts well to short periods of captivity.

forests, usually at higher altitudes, while the northern water shrew will only be found along wooded mountain streams with heavy cover on the banks, and meadow jumping mice like damp fields and ferny woods. Before you start to trap, it is important to research what species are in your area, their habitat preferences, food habits and general life histories. This will help you catch them, and care for them properly once they are in captivity.

Nighttime is the most productive trapping period. In mild, dry weather, sitting overnight in the trap will not harm the captured animal, but in inclement weather, check the traps every two or three hours. This is especially important if you are trapping shrews, which have an exceptionally high metabolism and can literally starve to death overnight.

A large aquarium tank, equipped with a tightly fitting, screened top, makes the best temporary housing for small mammals. Cedar or pine shavings provide easily cleaned bedding, although you may want to add a section of log or branches, especially if the species likes to climb, such as a deer mouse or red-backed vole. Most

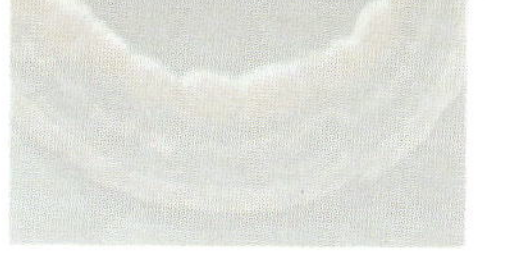

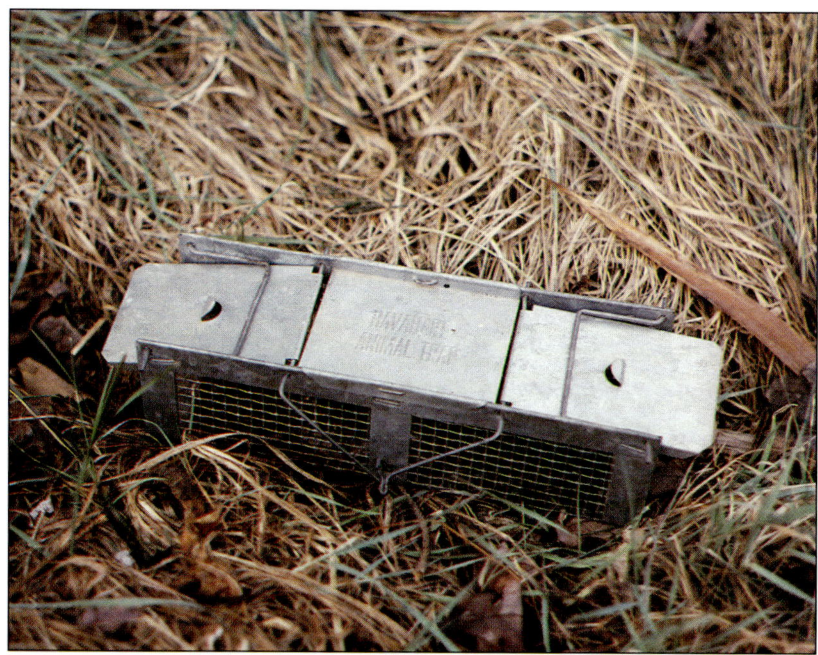

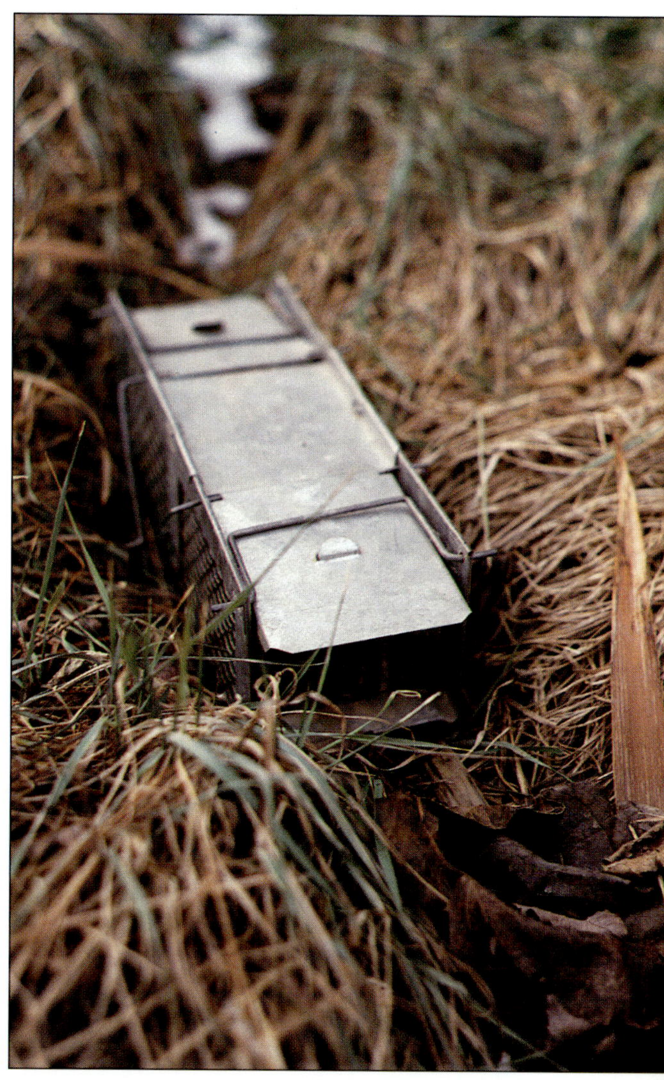

ABOVE AND RIGHT Set small live traps along runways and paths. For best results cover the trap with dead grass, but be sure the camouflage doesn't interfere with the operation of the trap.

importantly, provide a nest box – a small cardboard box with a hole cut in one side is fine – so the animal can hide when it wants to. This is essential; a small mammal that feels constantly exposed can actually die from the stress. Make sure water, supplied in a standard glass water bottle, is always available.

Diet will depend on the species. Deer mice, white-footed mice and their relatives will do fine on a mix of sunflower seed, millet, pieces of fruit and small amounts of raw meat, and may be weaned onto a commercial rodent diet. Meadow voles need a large percentage of fresh greens, while grasshopper mice of the West need quite a bit of meat to replace their natural diet of insects, lizards and other mice. Shrews, with their never-ending hunger and carnivorous habits, have the most exacting dietary requirements. Natural prey items like insects and earthworms are best, but a high-quality canned dog food is a good substitute, at least in the short-term.

Because most small mammals are shy and nocturnal, it is best to observe them at night, even in captivity. A red light bulb – the light of which is visible to human eyes but almost invisible to theirs – allows you watch without disturbing your charges.

While it is best to release the mammals after several weeks, you may wish to keep one or two for long-term study. Release the animal in the same habitat – preferably the same spot – where it was caught. Jumping mice, which pass the winter in hibernation, require special consideration. To maintain captive jumping mice over the winter, provide a large (55 gallon or bigger) terrarium almost filled with soil, and allow them to dig hibernacula chambers. Store the tank in a location where the temperature will stay between 32 and 40°F throughout the winter. Perhaps the safest course is to release any captive jumping mice by late August, so they can hibernate in the wild.

INTERPRETING ANIMAL BEHAVIOR

RECOMMENDED EQUIPMENT
- Binoculars
- Field notebook
- Blind (if necessary)

For a beginning naturalist, the greatest pleasure comes from finding and identifying new things – unusual birds, rare wildflowers, new butterflies. And with good reason, for identification is the first step on the path to understanding. But there inevitably comes a time when simply ticking off new species loses its appeal, and the naturalist looks for another challenge.

One of the most rewarding is observing, recording and interpreting animal behavior. The dedicated amateur can make substantial contributions to our knowledge of natural history – and it isn't necessary to travel to distant parts of the globe to do so. Many of the most common animals have never been studied in depth, and much of how they live their lives and interact with each other is mystery.

A bird feeder is a great place to start, since it draws large numbers of individuals, and you can watch from comfort and hiding – the latter an important consideration, because the presence of a human will change an animal's natural behavior.

Eventually you'll want to keep notes on what you see, but for the time being, just watch. Become familiar with the comings and goings of the birds, the pecking order at the feeder. Who gives the first alarm when a sharp-shinned hawk or a cat comes near? Which is the first to return when the danger is past? Which species feed on the ground, which on the feeder – which close to cover, which farther away? At all times, keep the paramount question in your mind: Why? Interpreting animal behavior is an art that blends observation, researched information and the ability to guess at another species' motives.

Any place where animals gather regularly, especially parks, refuges and other areas where they are habituated to human presence, are good locations for watching behavior. The spring and summer are particularly rewarding times of the year, when birds and mammals are busy courting and rearing young. It is important, however, to keep the welfare of the animal foremost; nest-watching, for instance, can cause serious disturbance and run the risk of attracting predators, and so should be avoided unless the nest can be watched from inside a building.

Neither should you confine your attentions to the higher vertebrates. Butterflies, for instance, have a complex social life that includes territories, pecking orders, courtship flights and battles between rival males. The breeding behavior of frogs and toads,

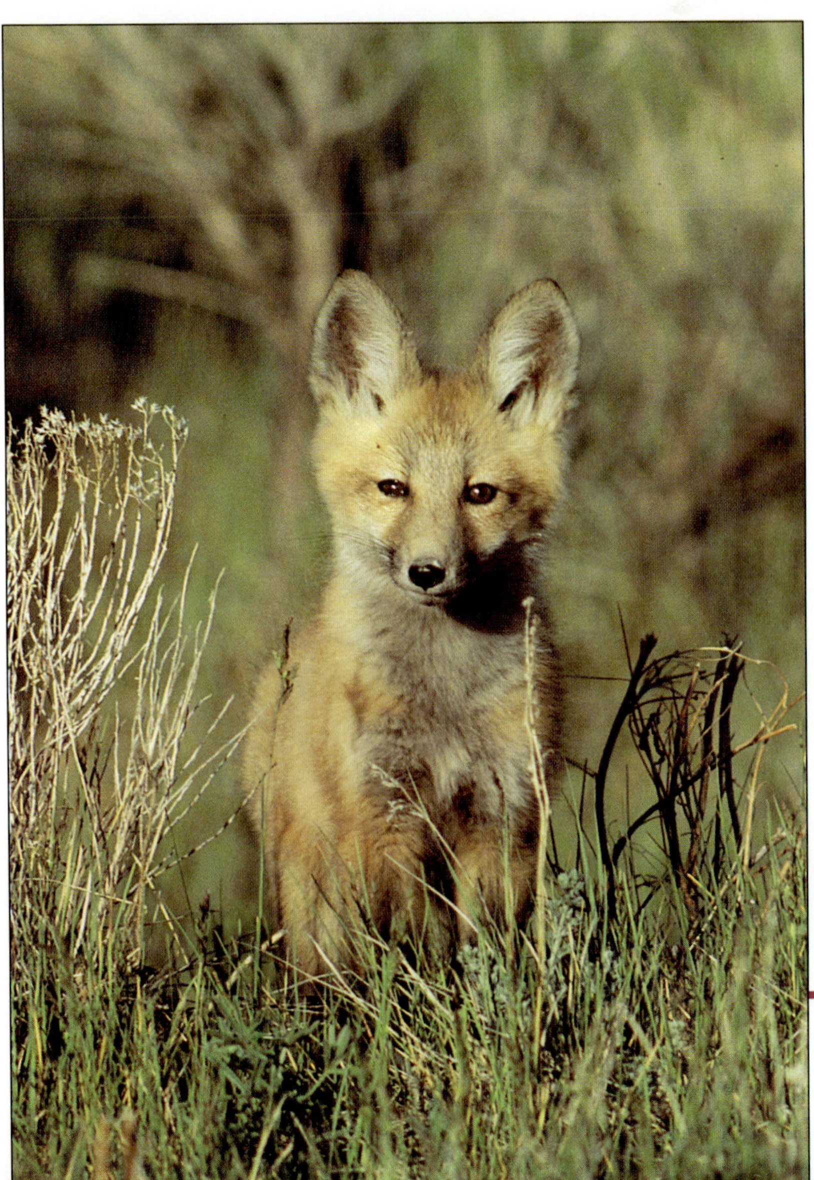

BELOW Observing animals at the den or nest, like this red fox pup near its den in Montana, is rewarding, but care must be taken not to disturb the animals in the process.

viewed at night by flashlight, is fascinating. Fish are another subject worthy of study; a researcher in Pennsylvania made some astonishing discoveries about dominance and hierarchy among brown trout by patiently watching a stretch of stream from a tower. He told individual trout apart by the unique patterns of spots on their backs.

The hardest part about interpreting animal behavior is avoiding anthropomorphism – reading human emotions into animal behavior. Animals are not little people wearing fur and feathers, and they live their lives in very different ways. Watching a flock of pheasants harass one of its members because she lost a foot to a hay mower, and walks with a limp, is unpleasant, but do not make value judgments. Instinct plays a far greater role in an animal's life than emotion; a hawk gently brooding her chick in the nest can be seen as an act of love, but what if the chick falls to the ground? The same solicitous female may kill and eat it, not out of hatred or anger, but because her instinctive reaction is to brood any small, moving shape in her nest, but to hunt any small, moving shape outside of it.

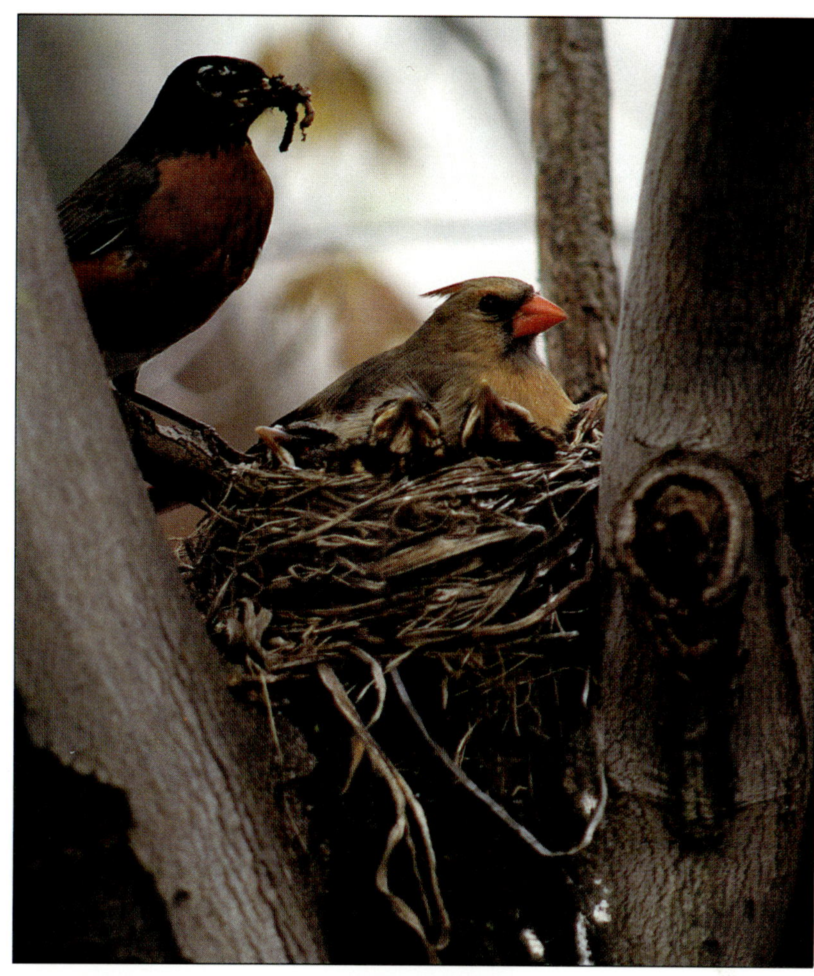

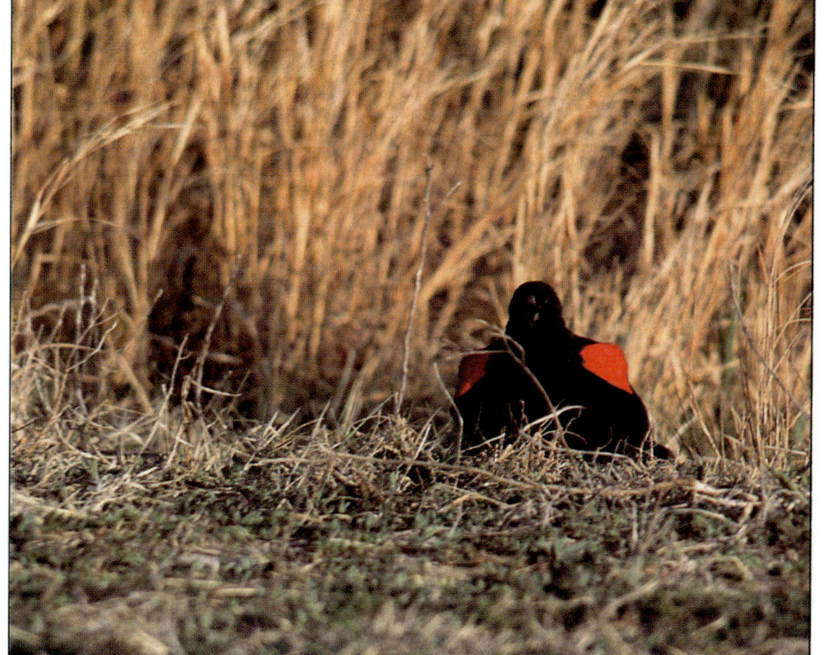

RIGHT A male red-winged blackbird flashes his fiery epaulets in a challenge to other male blackbirds intruding in his territory.

ABOVE Behavioral oddities can be especially interesting – and poignant. This female cardinal "adopted" a nest of baby robins after her own nest was destroyed, and helped the adults care for the chicks. The male robin waits with a beakful of food while his mate is away hunting.

FOSSIL HUNTING

RECOMMENDED EQUIPMENT

- Hand lens
- Rock hammer
- Work gloves
- Collecting bags and rucksack

With the gentle tap of a hammer, the chunk of rock splits neatly in your hand into two slabs. Inside, impressed in perfect detail on each half, is the form of a shell – the fossil of a long-extinct animal, exposed to the light of day for the first time in millions of years.

Fossil hunting carries the thrill of time-travel, resurrecting from dead stone the history of life on Earth. Each fossil is a verse in a greater chapter; each testifies eloquently to a world very different from our own.

In a good fossil bed the ground can seem literally carpeted with fossils, but the circumstances that allow a dead creature to be immortalized in rock are so rare and precise that it has been called a miracle that any fossils form at all. The vast majority of ancient animals and plants died and decomposed without leaving any trace of their existence. A very, very few, however, wound up in the right place at the right time – buried in fine sediment that excluded oxygen (and aerobic bacteria), undisturbed by geological upheaval as the sediment turned to rock, and as minerals replaced the organic structure of the once-living thing molecule by molecule.

If all goes right, the end result is a fossil – a mineralized reminder of what once was. Generally, only the hard parts are fossilized – bones, teeth, shells and the like, although under the right conditions, plants and even soft-bodied invertebrates can be fossilized. There are fossil insects, trapped in tree resin that mineralized into amber, even coprolites – fossilized animal dung.

In most areas, the common fossils are sea creatures and plants, however. The most rewarding hunting will come in fossil beds, layers of sedimentary rock that hold

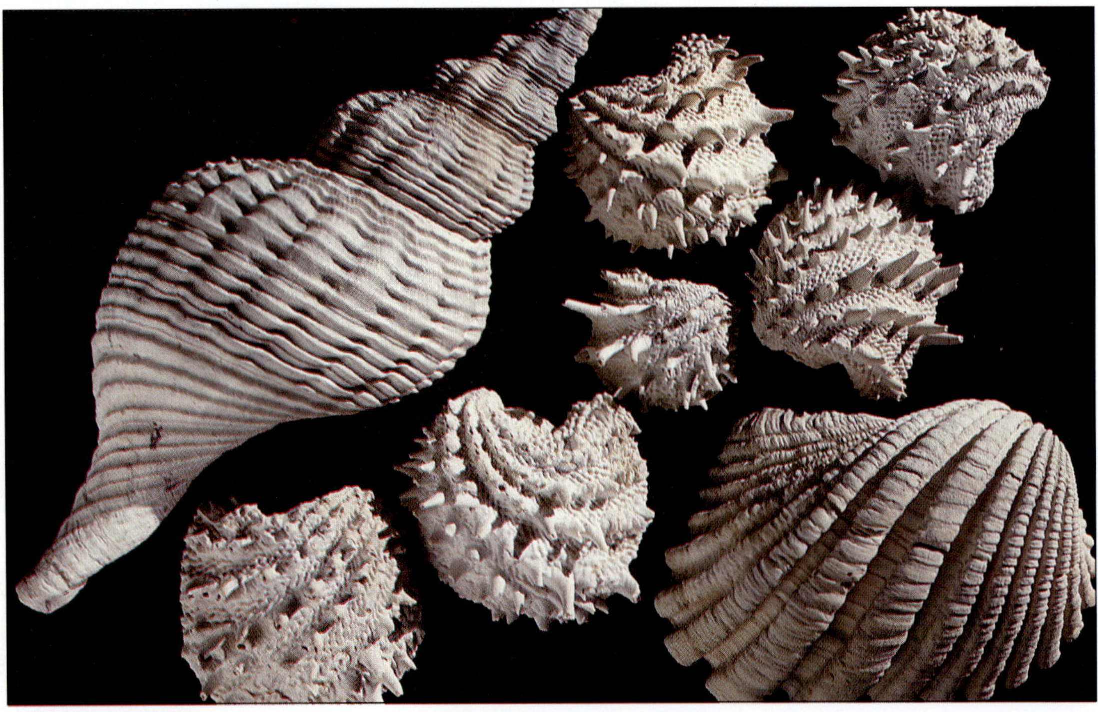

RIGHT A variety of marine fossils from Florida.

COMMON FOSSILS

Trilobites – One of the best-known fossils, trilobites are named for the three-fold organization of their bodies. Dating from the Cambrian Period some 500 million years ago, trilobites were bottom feeders.

Brachiopods – Also known as lamp shells, brachiopods are extremely common in Paleozoic rocks. At first glance they resemble clams or scallops, although they were anchored to the bottom by a muscular foot.

Crinoids – The most common fossil of a crinoid is its segmented stem, although occasionally one will find its feathery arms and rootlike holdfasts, all of which make this sea animal look very much like a plant. Like the brachiopods, some crinoid species survive to this day, although most are free-swimming instead of sedentary.

Sharks' teeth – Common along many Florida beaches, the sheer number of fossil teeth staggers the mind – until one realizes that each shark grows and sheds hundreds of teeth in its lifetime. Teeth, because they are clad in hard enamel, are among the most frequently fossilized body parts.

Ferns and plants – Most plant fossils date from the swampy Carboniferous Period, some 310 million years ago, and are found in coal-bearing strata, although the fossils themselves are generally in shale. Many have a glossy sheen over the impression – the organic remains of the plant itself.

an abundance of fossils; such beds are usually well-known, and a list may be available from state or provincial geological surveys. Construction and development are constantly unearthing new sites, however, so it pays to check highway cuts and other areas where sedimentary rock is being exposed. Naturally, be sure to have permission before entering private property, and stay away from active construction sites.

Fossil hunting is a game of the eye. Human activity and natural weathering will have exposed many fossils, and careful use of a rock hammer will produce more. Some rocks, like shale, can be gingerly split into thinner leaves, revealing fossils in between. In most cases there will be two impressions – the "part," or the specimen itself, and the "counterpart," the negative cast in the surrounding rock.

For common fossils like brachiopods, shark teeth, trilobites and ferns, there is little danger that collecting by amateurs will result in the loss of scientifically important specimens. But the lay collector must know when to stand back and call in professionals. In the American and Canadian West in particular, there is the chance that an amateur fossil hunter will stumble across the remains of something important, like the fossil bones of a dinosaur. In such instances, the nonprofessional will do more harm than good should he or she disturb the fossil. Instead, contact the paleontology department of a local university for guidance.

When collecting, exercise restraint and show consideration for those who will come after you. Fossils are not a renewable resource, and deposits should be treated with care and respect.

BELOW Several common fossils: clockwise from top right, ferns, a brachiopod, a crinoid stem, ferns and an assortment of brachiopod shells.

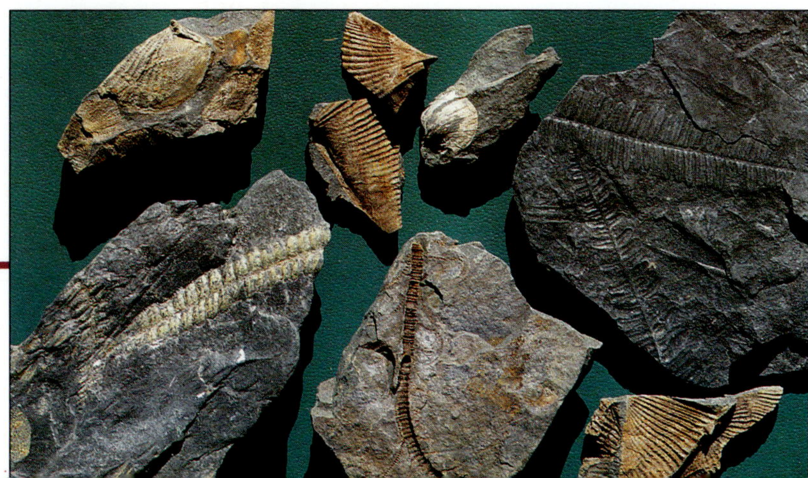

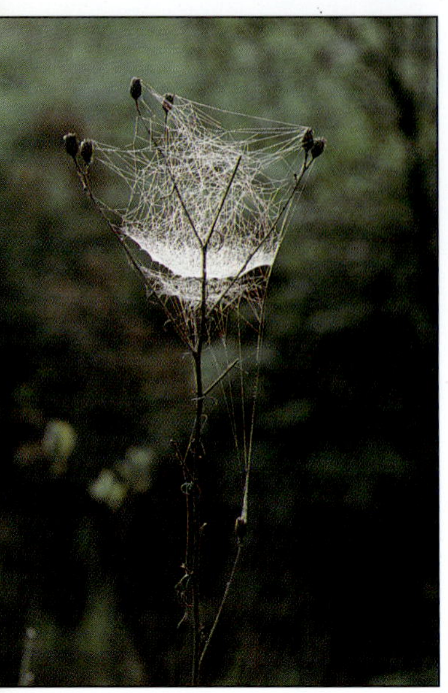

ABOVE A heavy summer dew – condensed here on a spider's web – is usually an indication of a clear, dry day ahead.

BECOMING A WEATHER-WATCHER

RECOMMENDED EQUIPMENT

- Thermometer
- Barometer
- Homemade wind gauge

Weather exerts a profound influence on everyone's life. In this day of satellite photography, radar and computer modeling, forecasting the weather has become an exact science – and a mystery to the average person.

But with a little attention to the sky, some simple meteorological instruments and a basic knowledge of how the atmosphere works, anybody can make short-term forecasts without ever tuning in to the news. In the process, one gains a much greater appreciation for the forces that power the Earth's weather.

In North America, weather systems march across the continent in a west-to-east pattern, with rare exceptions. Each system may be high atmospheric pressure (ordinarily bringing fair weather) or low pressure (generally bringing unsettled weather). In a high, wind circulates in a clockwise direction; as a high moves into the Northeast, for instance, the winds shift first out of the northwest, bringing in cooler air from Canada. As the high passes over, the winds may falter and die, only to pick up again as the high moves offshore – but blowing this time from the southwest, bringing up warmer, moister air. If the high stalls offshore in summer, the result is a heat wave.

Highs usually alternate with lows, in which the wind blows counterclockwise. Lows tend to have unsettled, unstable air laden with moisture, and are usually warmer than highs. When a high and low collide, the colder, high-pressure air triggers precipitation, since cooler air cannot hold as much water vapor as warmer air.

You can trace the comings and goings of pressure cells by using a barometer, which measures atmospheric pressure in inches of mercury; a steady or rising barometer indicates an approaching high, while a falling barometer signals a low. A good quality thermometer and a simple wind gauge would round out a home weather station. The wind gauge can be nothing more than a plywood arrowhead, balanced upright on a nail pivot at the end of a pole; erect the gauge away from buildings, trees and other windbreaks.

The most important tool may well be your eyes. Train yourself to be aware of cloud types and their direction, which indicate winds aloft (often different from ground winds). High, wispy cirrus clouds frequently presage an approaching low, while puffy cumulus clouds are the usual result of bright sun shining on cool, high-pressure air masses. In summer, those same cumulus clouds may grow to form cumulonimbus – thunderheads that may spawn lightning and heavy rain.

TEMPERATURE TIP

If you don't have a thermometer handy, you can still tell the temperature by listening to the chirps of a cricket. Count the number of chirps in 15 seconds and add 37 to determine the temperature – at least where the cricket is sitting – in Fahrenheit. Why does it work? Because the cricket, being a cold-blooded animal, functions at a pace directly tied to the air temperature.

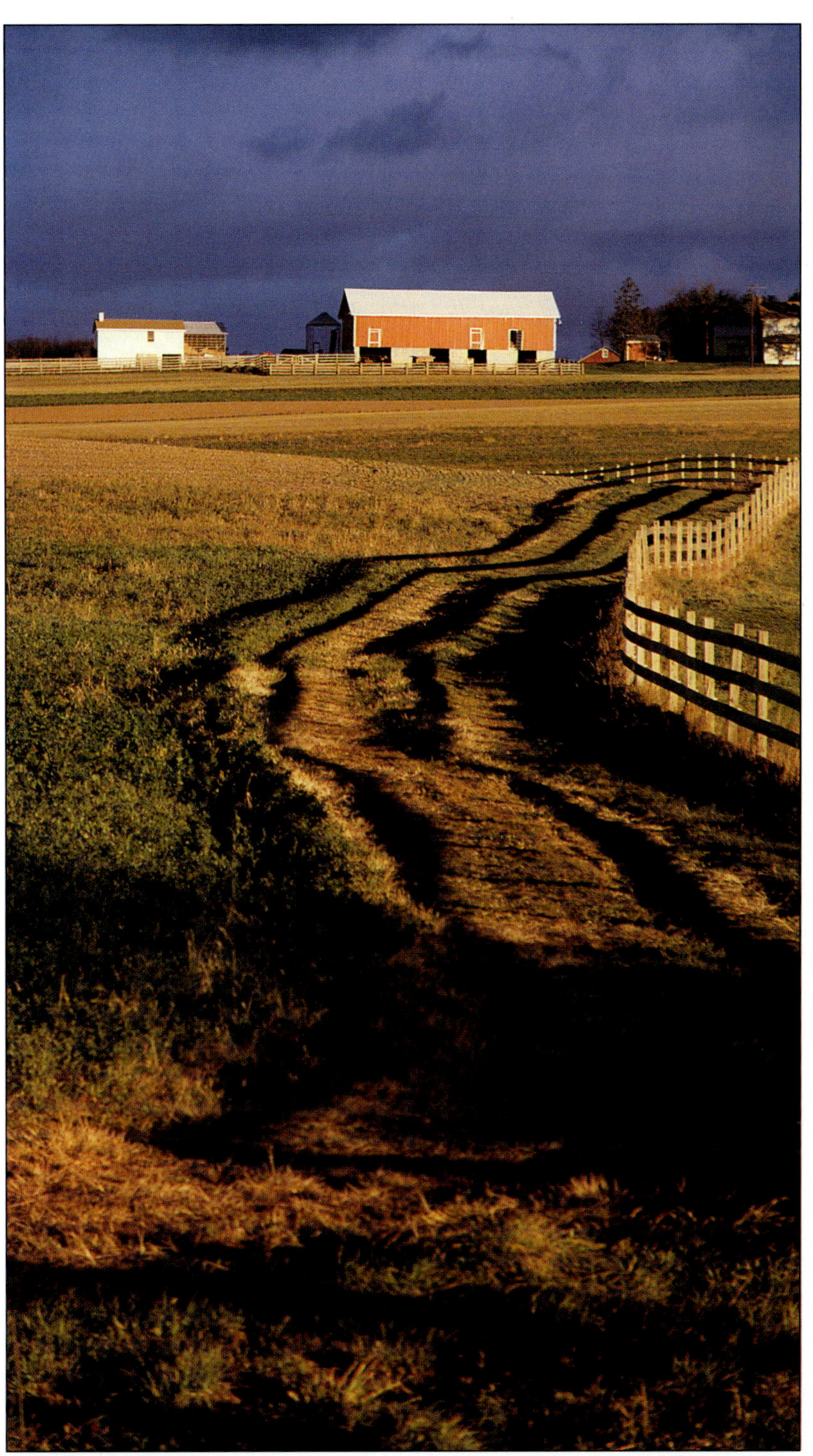

ABOVE With a basic understanding of how weather systems function, you can make an educated guess about upcoming weather from cloud patterns, wind direction and barometric pressure.

WEATHER FOLKLORE

People predicted the weather centuries before meteorology became a science. Here are a few old "rules of thumb," which will obviously not be accurate in every situation.

A ring around the moon means rain or snow. High altitude ice particles cause the ring, which forecasts precipitation about half the time.

Fog before seven, fair by eleven. In high pressure, morning fog usually means a fair day.

If wild animals are feeding heavily during the day in winter, expect a snow. Animals can sense falling atmospheric pressure, which often sparks a flurry of activity.

No morning dew in summer means rain.

A full moon brings frost. Meteorologists say there is no connection, but farmers get nervous during the full moon anyway.

Mare's tails and mackerel scales bring rain. High cirrus clouds (which often resemble flowing horse tails or fish scales) precede lows.

If bubbles in a cup of coffee join in the middle expect fair weather; if they make a ring around the cup rim, expect rain.

WATCHING METEOR SHOWERS

RECOMMENDED EQUIPMENT

- Binoculars
- Lawn chair
- Camera and tripod (for photographs)

Arcing across the night sky in a sliver of brilliant light, a meteor lasts but a moment. On a normal night, five or six an hour can be seen, the fallout of Earth's passage through the cosmos.

But periodically during the year, the Earth crosses the paths of comets – paths strewn with fine bits of grit and minerals. Caught in our planet's gravity, these particles are pulled down to their doom, lighting the sky with a meteor shower. The Leonid shower in November, for example, is caused by debris from Halley's Comet.

The timing of meteor showers is predictable, and although a shower may vary in quality from year to year, astronomers know that some showers will produce more than others. The most famous of them is the Perseid shower, which peaks on August 11, and has a frequency of about 50 to 60 meteors per hour. In the case of the Perseids, the meteoroids (as those still in space are known) are strung out rather uniformly along the path of Comet 1862 III. In the Leonid shower, which falls around Nov. 16, the meteoroids are bunched together on the comet's old path. When the Earth last smacked into the pack, in 1966, the rate of visible meteors was an astonishing 140 per *second*.

Meteors are space debris, fragments of iron, silicates and nickel, and collide with the Earth's atmosphere at a rate of some 25 million per day. Most are invisible, either because they strike during daylight, or because they are so small that their glow is too faint to be seen. Those that are larger (about 100th of an ounce) and fall at night can, however, be seen by anyone within about 100 miles. Occasionally, much bigger meteors come crashing down; more than 30 tons of meteoric debris has been found in the Barringer Meteorite Crater in Arizona, some 1,400 yards wide, and an ancient crater in Quebec is more than two miles across. Another meteoric impact in Quebec left a ring lake 40 miles wide.

The most famous meteorite fall in recorded history actually wasn't, it is now thought. In 1908, a tremendous explosion rocked Siberia, centered on a remote corner of the Tunguska River, leveling trees over a 750 square mile area. Once blamed on a meteorite, the explosion is now thought to have occurred when a comet about the size of a building hit the Earth, vaporizing just above the ground. The explosive force has been estimated at the equivalent of 12 megatons of TNT.

Interestingly, meteor showers, born of comets, never produce meteorites – perhaps because the particle size is uniformly small. The showers do produce spectacular viewing. The best time is after midnight, when your side of the Earth is facing directly into the old cometary path, and the best place is somewhere far from city lights, where the sky is blackest. Sit on a lawn chair or blanket, facing the "radiant" of the shower – the area of the sky from which the meteors appear, which in the case of the Perseids is the constellation Perseus in the northeastern sky. Binoculars can be a help, but your own eyes are best, especially once they have adjusted to the darkness and can pick out faint meteors.

To photograph meteors, use a 35mm camera with a wide-angle lens, mounted on a sturdy tripod. Set the focus to infinity, and the aperture wide open, and aim just to one side of the radiant. Using a locking cable release, trip the shutter (first lock the mirror in the up position, if your camera has this feature). The minimum exposure time should be about 15 minutes, and can be as long as four hours. As the Earth rotates the stars will leave curving paths, while meteor trails will be straight, white lines.

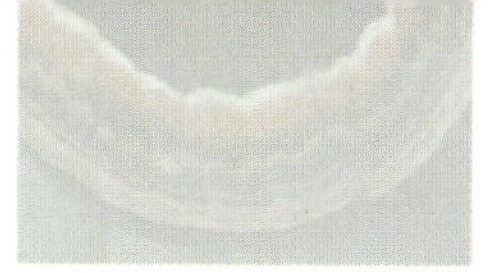

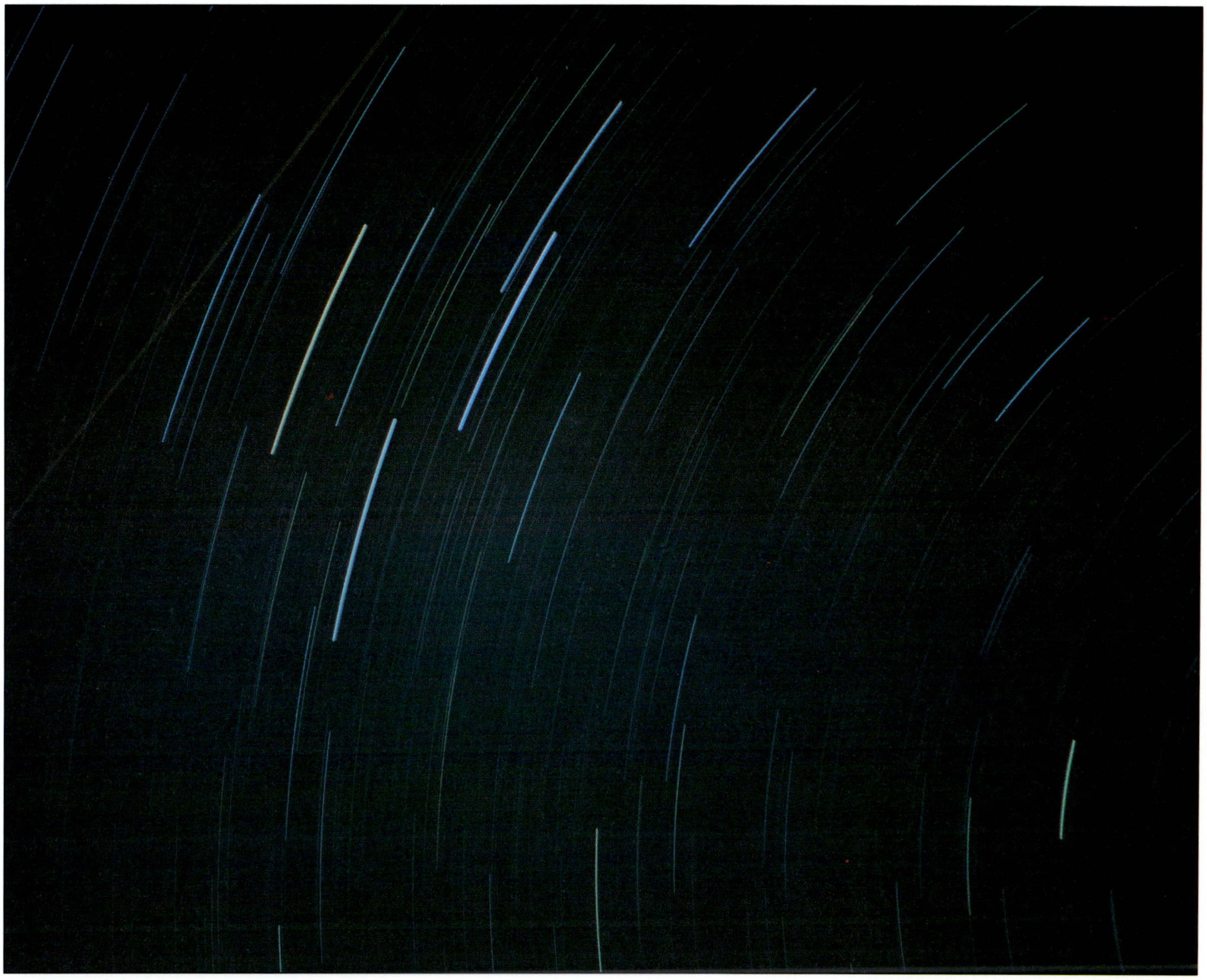

ABOVE A camera set to capture the streaks of meteors often catches unintended images instead – in this case, the passage of an airplane against star trails in a 20-minute time exposure.

MAJOR METEOR SHOWERS

NAME	PEAK	VISIBLE METEORS/HOUR	RADIANT
Quadrantid	Jan. 3	40	Between Bootes and Big Dipper
Perseid	Aug. 11	50-60	Perseus
Orionid	Oct. 20	25	Orion
Leonid	Nov. 16	Varies	Leo
Geminid	Dec. 13	50	Gemini
Ursid	Dec. 22	15	Big Dipper

CHAPTER FOUR

Advanced Techniques

PREPARING MUSEUM STUDY SKINS

RECOMMENDED EQUIPMENT

- Scalpel or sharp utility knife
- Tweezers
- Bulk cotton
- Sewing needles
- Nylon thread
- Light-gauge metal wire
- Latex gloves

Animals are best studied in the wild, but it is often helpful to be able to examine them in the hand, as well. For centuries, scientists have recognized the value of stuffed specimens, known as study skins.

Study skins can be important learning tools in the classroom, nature center or camp, but their preparation and possession are carefully regulated by law, with stiff fines for violations. Federal rules prohibit the possession (for any reason) of all but a few wild birds, and most mammals are protected by state or provincial laws. Check with your local wildlife conservation officer before proceeding, since special permits may be available for legitimate educational purposes.

Although the preparation of study skins uses many taxidermy techniques, the aim is not to prepare a lifelike mount, but simply one that displays characteristic plumage or color. A bird is stuffed on its back, wings folded and legs crossed, while mammals are stretched on their stomach, legs straight. Glass eyes are not used. A tag attached to the leg gives complete information about where and when the specimen was found. Virtually all specimens are "salvaged," that is, found dead – birds that hit windows or high-tension towers, mammals that are killed on the road.

The art shows the procedure for skinning and stuffing a small mammal. Make a single incision from the vent halfway up the belly, being careful not to slice through the abdominal wall. Work the hind legs free, cutting through the bone just above the foot. The tail nerve must be removed from the tail skin; on small animals pinch the thumb and forefinger nails against the nerve to hold the skin in place, then pull the nerve out gently.

The skin comes off like a sock, inside out. Free the forelegs, again cutting the leg bones just above the feet so the feet remain attached to the skin. Go slowly at the head, cutting the ears free close to the skull. Use short slices, close to the bone, to free the eyelids and lips, then cut the nose free.

Using the skinned body as a guide, create a body form of cotton, wrapped tightly with thread to stiffen it, duplicating the animal's shape and dimensions as closely as possible. Insert a length of wire, well wrapped with cotton if necessary, to replace the tail nerve. Use wisps of cotton, inserted with forceps, to fill in any gaps. Sew up the incision from the vent forward, using small, tight stitches.

Stretch the finished study skin out on

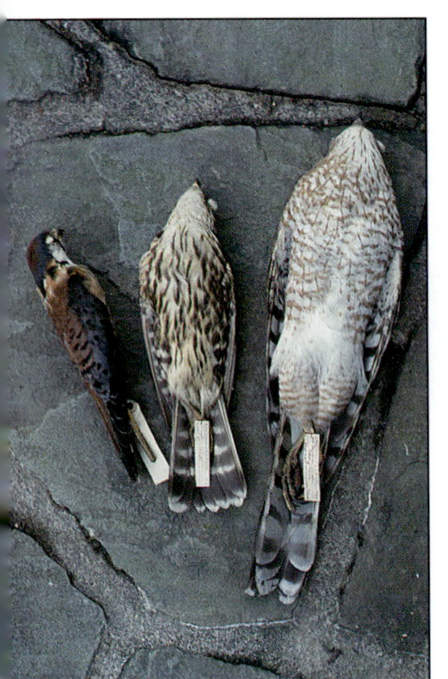

ABOVE Properly prepared and stored, study skins can last for centuries. These – an American kestrel, a merlin and a Cooper's hawk – date from the late 19th century.

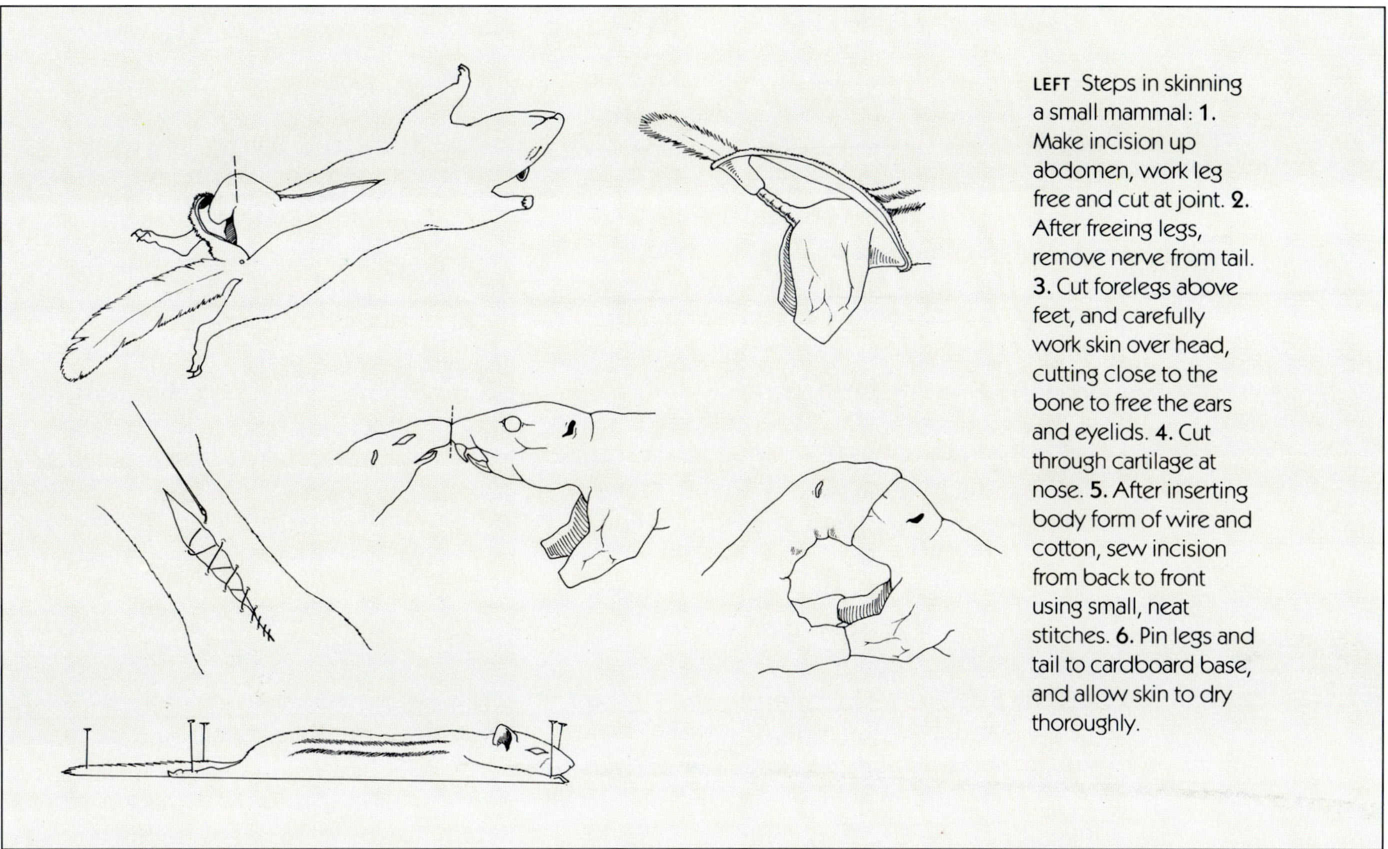

LEFT Steps in skinning a small mammal: **1.** Make incision up abdomen, work leg free and cut at joint. **2.** After freeing legs, remove nerve from tail. **3.** Cut forelegs above feet, and carefully work skin over head, cutting close to the bone to free the ears and eyelids. **4.** Cut through cartilage at nose. **5.** After inserting body form of wire and cotton, sew incision from back to front using small, neat stitches. **6.** Pin legs and tail to cardboard base, and allow skin to dry thoroughly.

heavy cardboard, pinning the legs in position until dry – a process that will take several days to a week, depending on the humidity.

Birds are prepared in much the same way, with a few important differences. Cut the tail free from the body just ahead of the base of the feathers. The wings are only skinned out to the first joint (the "elbow," if you will), and the skull must be thoroughly cleaned and reinserted into the skin, with cotton in the eye sockets and skull cavity; remove the brain through a rectangular hole cut in the rear of the skull. Use extreme care in skinning birds, because most have tissue-thin skin that tears easily.

CAUTION

Working with dead animals presents an obvious health risk, albeit a rather small one since few animal diseases are communicable to humans. Choose only specimens that are freshly killed (limp muscles and flexible joints are a good sign), and do not use animals that you know were acting oddly before dying. Wear latex surgical gloves at all times, and do not handle a dead animal if you have open wounds on your hands. After preparing a specimen, discard the gloves and wash your hands thoroughly with hot water and an antiseptic soap. If your area is experiencing a rabies outbreak, it is best to avoid mammalian specimens entirely.

BELOW Tools for study skin preparation – small scissors, forceps, a sharp utility knife, thread and needle, and cotton.

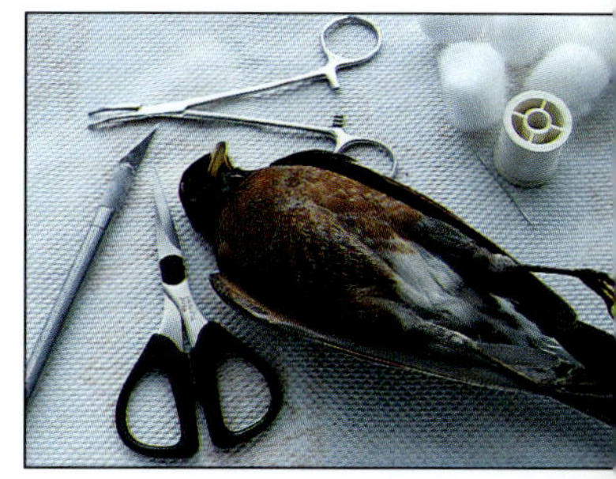

CARING FOR WILDLIFE INFANTS

As a rule, wild animals do not make good pets; that baby raccoon that was so cute when it was two months old can be a destructive, biting menace when it grows up. For this very good reason, it is illegal to keep most wild mammals and all birds as pets. But what about the baby robins whose nest was blown apart by a thunderstorm? Or the gray squirrel infants whose nest tree was cut down by mistake?

More and more states and provinces are licensing trained wildlife rehabilitators to care for such animals. But if you cannot find a rehabilitator – and if you are willing to take on a great deal of responsibility – it may be necessary for you to care for orphaned or injured wildlife on an emergency basis.

BABY BIRDS – Most "orphaned" baby birds are nothing of the sort – they are chicks that have left the nest, but are not yet able to fly well, a very normal situation. Fledglings have short tails and flight feathers, and are still being cared for by their parents, who might not be in immediate attendance, however. Return fledglings to where they were found, and place them in a tree or bush. Don't worry about handling them; birds have little sense of smell, and the parents will not abandon them because they were touched by human hands.

Younger birds that cannot be placed back in the nest need two things – food and warmth. Line a berry basket with a towel to form a nest, and place a 40-watt light bulb nearby for warmth; the temperature should be around 80F, but can be reduced to room temperature as the chicks feather out. Avoid drafts.

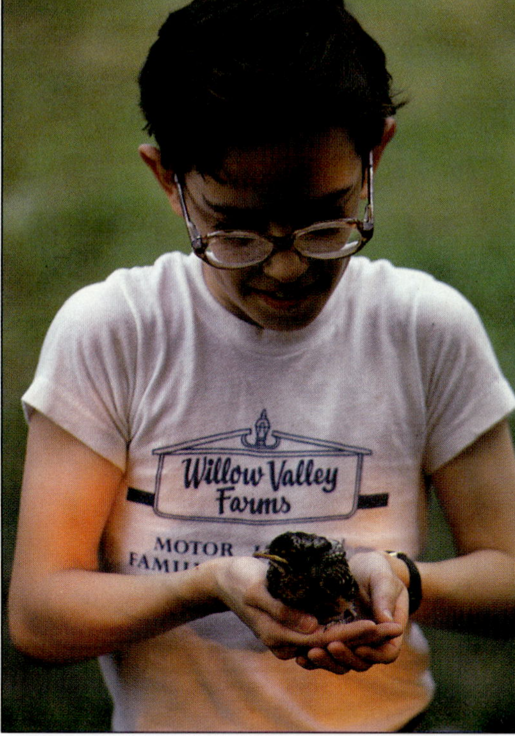

RIGHT As soon as a young bird is old enough to fly, it should be slowly weaned back to the outdoors and an independent life.

In the wild the parents would feed the chicks every few minutes from sunup to sundown. That is impractical for most people, so feed as much as the chicks will take once an hour (every half hour for very young, naked chicks). Perhaps the best captive diet is a high-grade canned dog food, dipped in whipped raw egg and fed in small pieces; keep the food refrigerated, but warm small quantities to room temperature before feeding. Place each morsel far back in the chick's throat, using a finger or a smooth, blunt instrument. Baby birds do not drink in the nest, so do not give water, which they may inhale with fatal results.

BABY MAMMALS – Food and warmth are again essential. Most young mammals will be chilled when found; warm them against your skin (inside a shirt), or with a

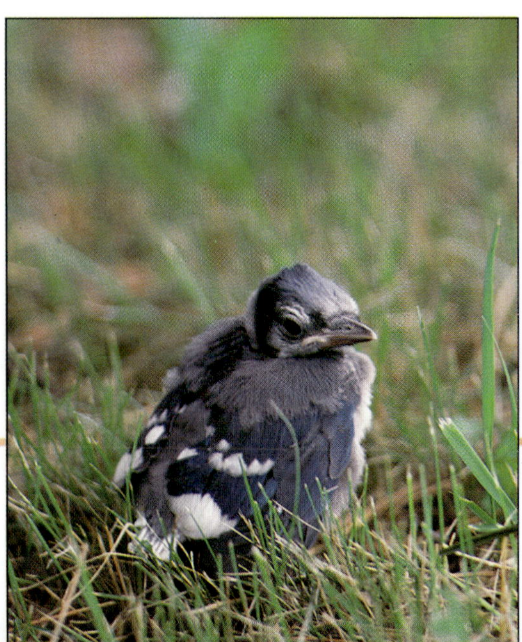

RIGHT A young blue jay, fresh out of its nest and unable to fly well, looks for all the world like an orphan – but it isn't, and like most wild babies it needs no help from people.

warm-water bottle or a heating pad set to the lowest setting before trying to feed. For hairless young, keep in a towel-lined nest box warmed by a light bulb to about 90°F. Older babies can be kept at 80F, then room temperature. Set the heat source at one end of the cage so they can crawl away if they become too warm.

Cow's milk is too rich for most wild mammals, and will cause fatal diarrhea. In a pinch, feed a mix of 1 cup water, a half-cup of canned, evaporated milk, and one egg yolk. Better is a mix of a third-cup Esbilac to a half-cup of water; weaken if the animal's stool is soft. Any formula should be warmed to skin temperature before feeding.

Feed about every three or four hours (every six hours for rabbits), holding the animal belly-down while you offer formula with a clean eyedropper. After feeding, it is essential that you stimulate defecation by gently stroking the animal's stomach and anus with a warm, wet washcloth, which replaces the mother's tongue. Babies not given this treatment will die of constipation. As they grow, offer adult food, allowing them to wean themselves at their own pace.

The death rate among wild orphans is very high, however good the care. Digestive problems in particular claim many, and are often not the fault of the person trying to raise the baby. Avoid problems by keeping all nesting areas and feeding utensils clean.

Wild infants of any sort – birds or mammals – should not be handled any more than absolutely necessary. This prevents stress, and will ease their eventual return to the wild. This final stage is always hardest on the humans, but it must be done. The best approach is a gradual one; set up a cage or nest box outside (a screened porch is ideal), allowing the babies more and more freedom over time, but providing a safe haven and food for as long as they need it. Eventually they will drift away, on their own at last.

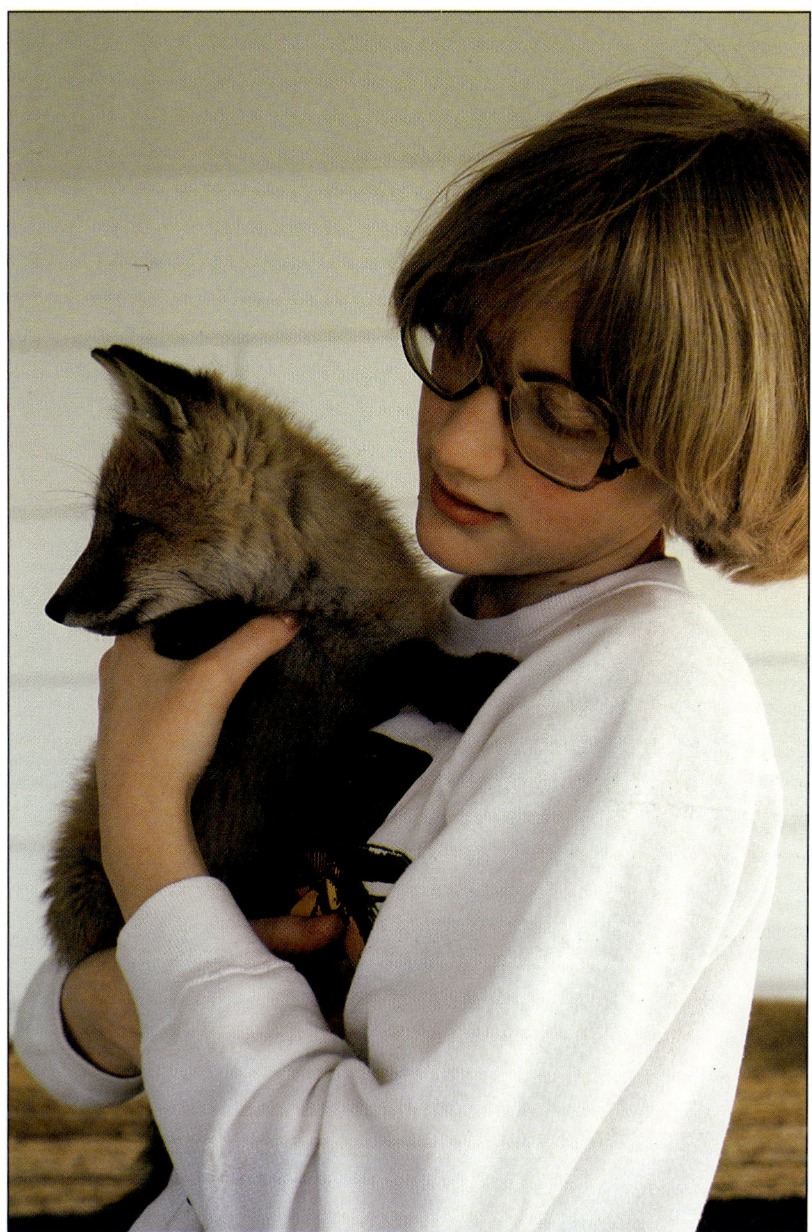

CAUTION

In areas where rabies is a problem, it is better not to handle any wild mammals, even infants. This may seem cold-hearted, but rabies is fatal and incurable, and can be transmitted from mother to offspring – and then to humans, however well-meaning. Better to play it safe.

ABOVE A baby red fox may look cute and cuddly, but when it grows up it will be aggressive and potentially dangerous – just one more reason why most wild animals do not make good pets.

BIRD BANDING

John James Audubon is credited with being the first bird-bander, ringing the legs of phoebe nestlings with silver wire. By doing so, he proved that birds return year after year to nest in the same place.

Banding today is far more sophisticated. Banders – licensed by the U.S. Fish and Wildlife Service or the Canadian Wildlife Service – annually band millions of songbirds, waterfowl, raptors and other species, helping science unlock the mysteries of birds' lives. Because of banding, we know about migration corridors and flyways, life spans, mating habits, home range and much, much more.

Because improper handling is dangerous to birds, banding is carefully regulated. Only licensed banders are permitted to trap and band birds; by law, applicants must be at least 18 years old, with a demonstrated proficiency in bird identification and the written endorsement of at least three licensed banders. In practical terms, only those working on research projects will be issued banding licenses. However, there are many banding projects around the U.S. and Canada that take on volunteer helpers. This way, interested individuals can work with trained banders, learning how to handle and process birds legally. Check with local conservation groups or wildlife refuges for more information about such projects.

Banders use a variety of traps to catch birds, banding them with light-weight aluminum rings issued by the government. Each is stamped with a sequential number, and the words "ADVISE BIRD BAND WRITE

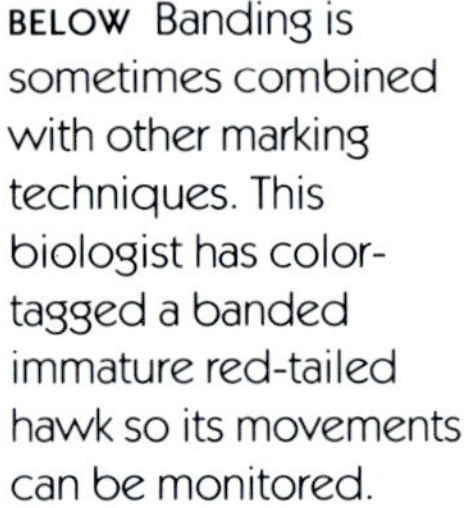

BELOW Banding is sometimes combined with other marking techniques. This biologist has color-tagged a banded immature red-tailed hawk so its movements can be monitored.

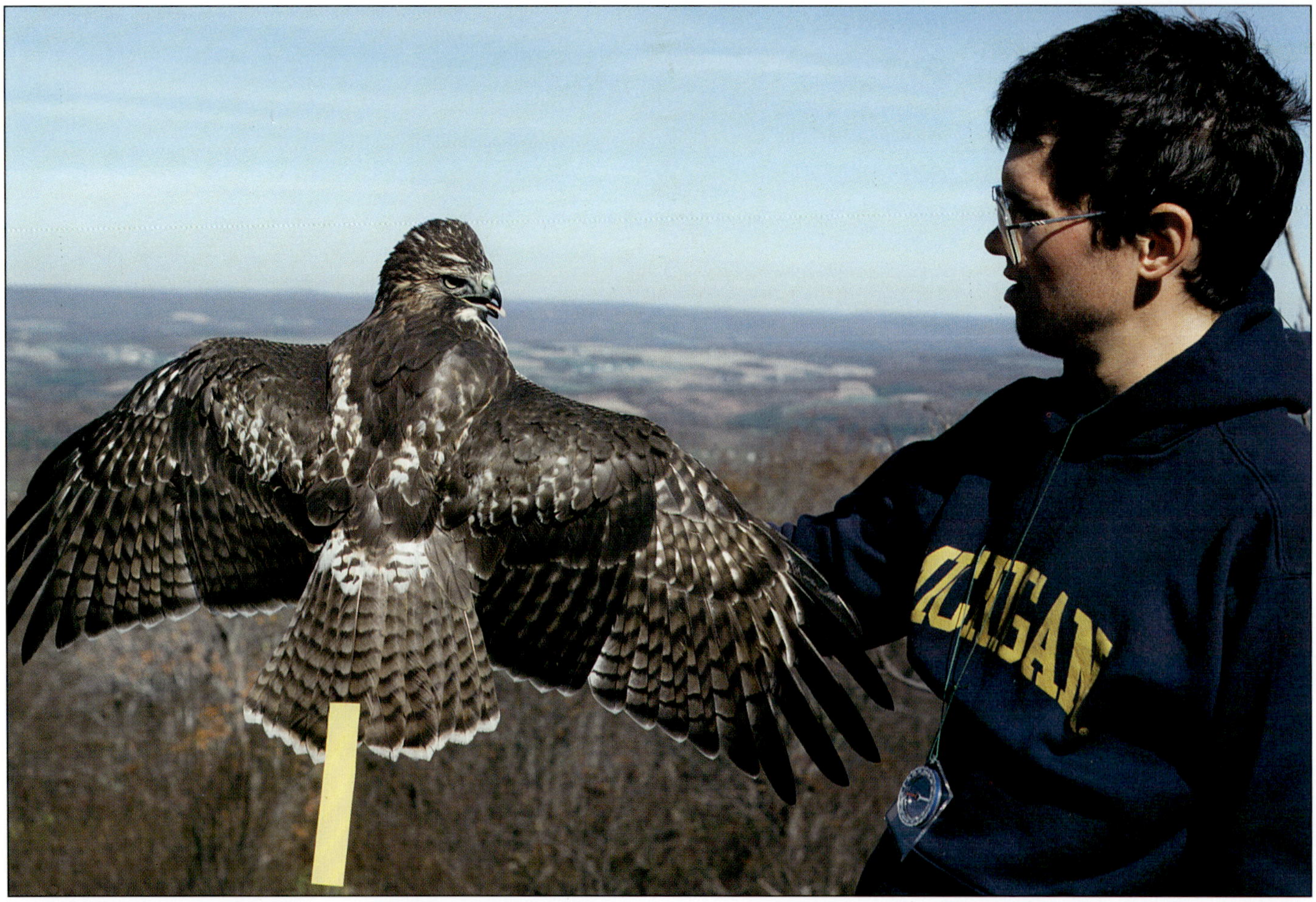

WASHINGTON D.C. USA." Using special pliers, the bander crimps the band loosely around the bird's leg; the band number, species, sex, age and other information is recorded on log sheets, and later entered into a computer. The band will stay on the bird throughout its life.

If you find a dead bird with a band, carefully write down the complete number (it is not necessary to remove the band), and send the information to: Bird Banding Laboratory, U.S. Fish and Wildlife Service, Laurel, MD 20708. Under no circumstances should you remove a band from a live bird, since it may be recaptured at a later date, affording even more information. The Bird Banding Lab serves as the repository for all North American banding information, and will send you a certificate detailing where, when and by whom the bird was banded.

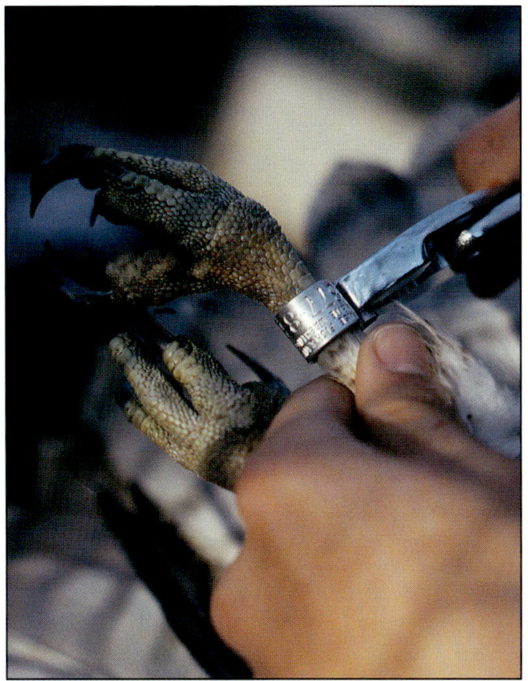

LEFT Using pliers, a bander crimps a numbered aluminum band on the leg of a young red-tailed hawk, captured during its fall migration. If the bird is ever found again, the band will tell scientists much about its life history and travels.

BELOW A red-shouldered hawk rests patiently as a bander records details of its age, size and weight before releasing it. Banding requires a federal permit and participation in an approved scientific study.

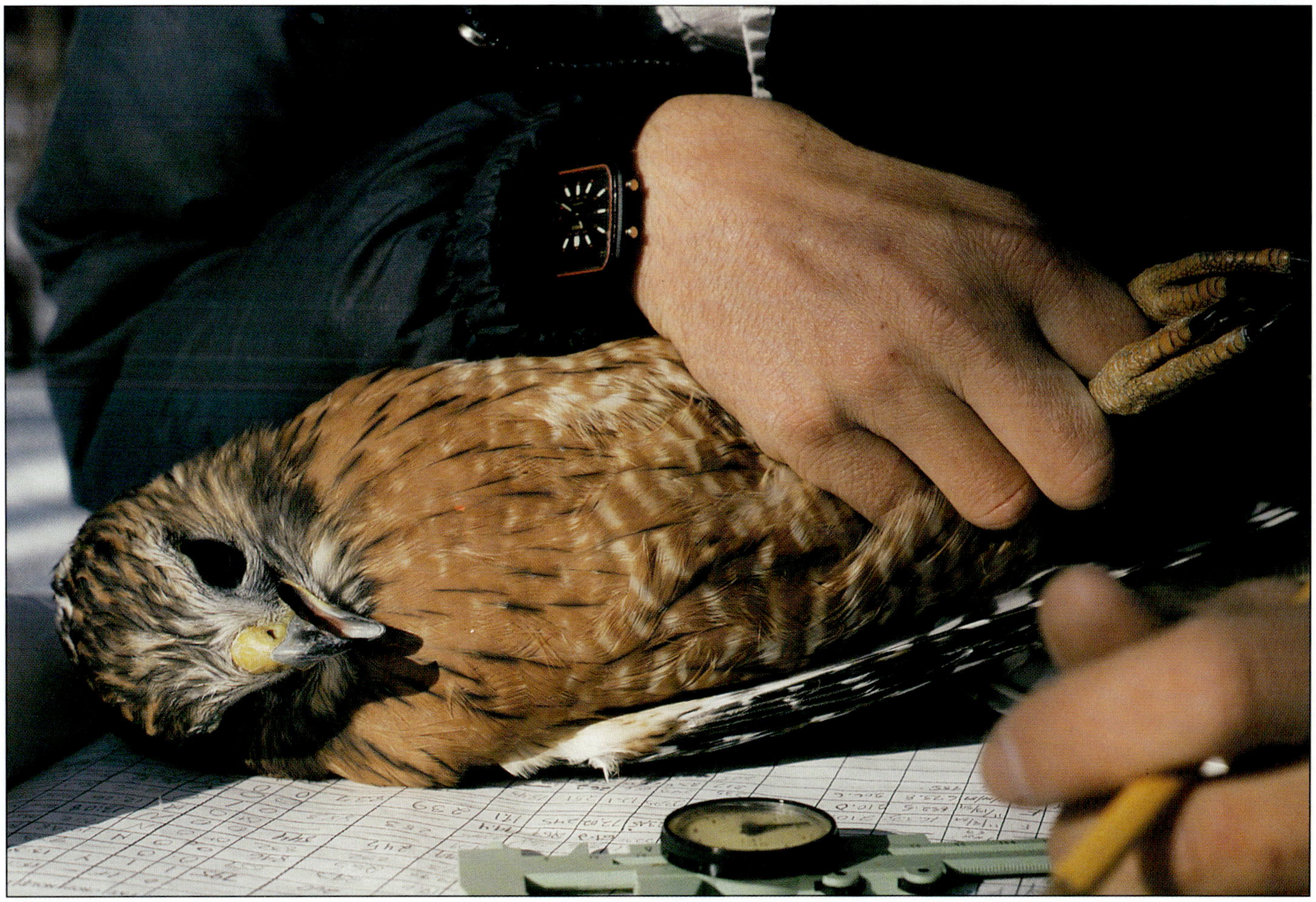

STARTING A SKULL COLLECTION

RECOMMENDED EQUIPMENT

- Hatchet
- Skinning tools
- Old pot for boiling
- Chlorine bleach or hydrogen peroxide
- Latex gloves

BELOW Unless the collection is for simple enjoyment, each skull should be labeled with the species, sex, date and location; the specimen number refers to a file entry that includes more detailed information.

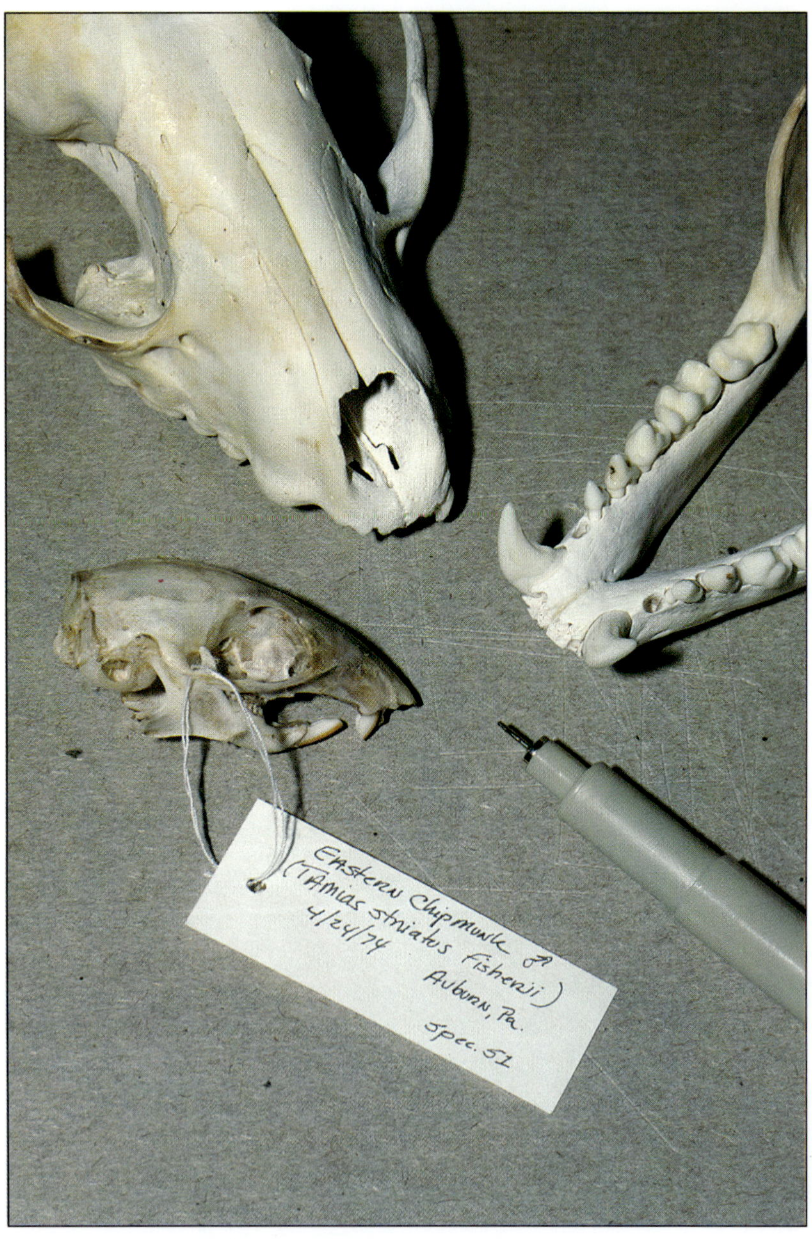

Skulls are among the biggest, thickest, hardest bones in the body, so it is no surprise that the naturalist will stumble across them from time to time in the field. Skulls are also a wealth of information about their previous owners – the placement of the eyes, the size and shape of the teeth, the size of the brain case, all speak volumes. Little wonder that many naturalists keep skull collections.

You can get skulls two ways – finding them afield, or preparing them from dead animals. Found skulls tend to be in poor condition; rodents may have gnawed at the bone for calcium, the teeth may be missing, and the bone may be soiled or broken. It takes a fair bit of work to turn a whole head into a clean skull, but that results in the best specimen.

As with the rest of these advanced techniques, be sure to check the law before proceeding. With the exception of gamebirds legally taken during hunting season, most bird skulls are taboo, just as are feathers or any other body parts. The rules vary widely on mammals, however, so ask your wildlife agency before going further. Also, the same health cautions mentioned for study skins apply here, and latex gloves are recommended when handling fresh specimens.

Thanks to the automobile, there is an abundance of road-killed animals from which to chose. Obviously, avoid specimens that suffered head injuries. Take the animal away from the road, and cut off the head with a hatchet, being careful not to damage the skull. At home, skin it and remove as much flesh as possible, being careful to avoid cutting the bone. Use a hooked wire (a hairpin will do) to remove the brain through the spinal cord hole at the back of the skull.

When most of the flesh is removed, gently boil the skull, then pick off the cooked meat. Do this step outside on a camp stove, since the smell is usually unpleasant. An alternative, especially with small skulls, is to remove as much flesh as

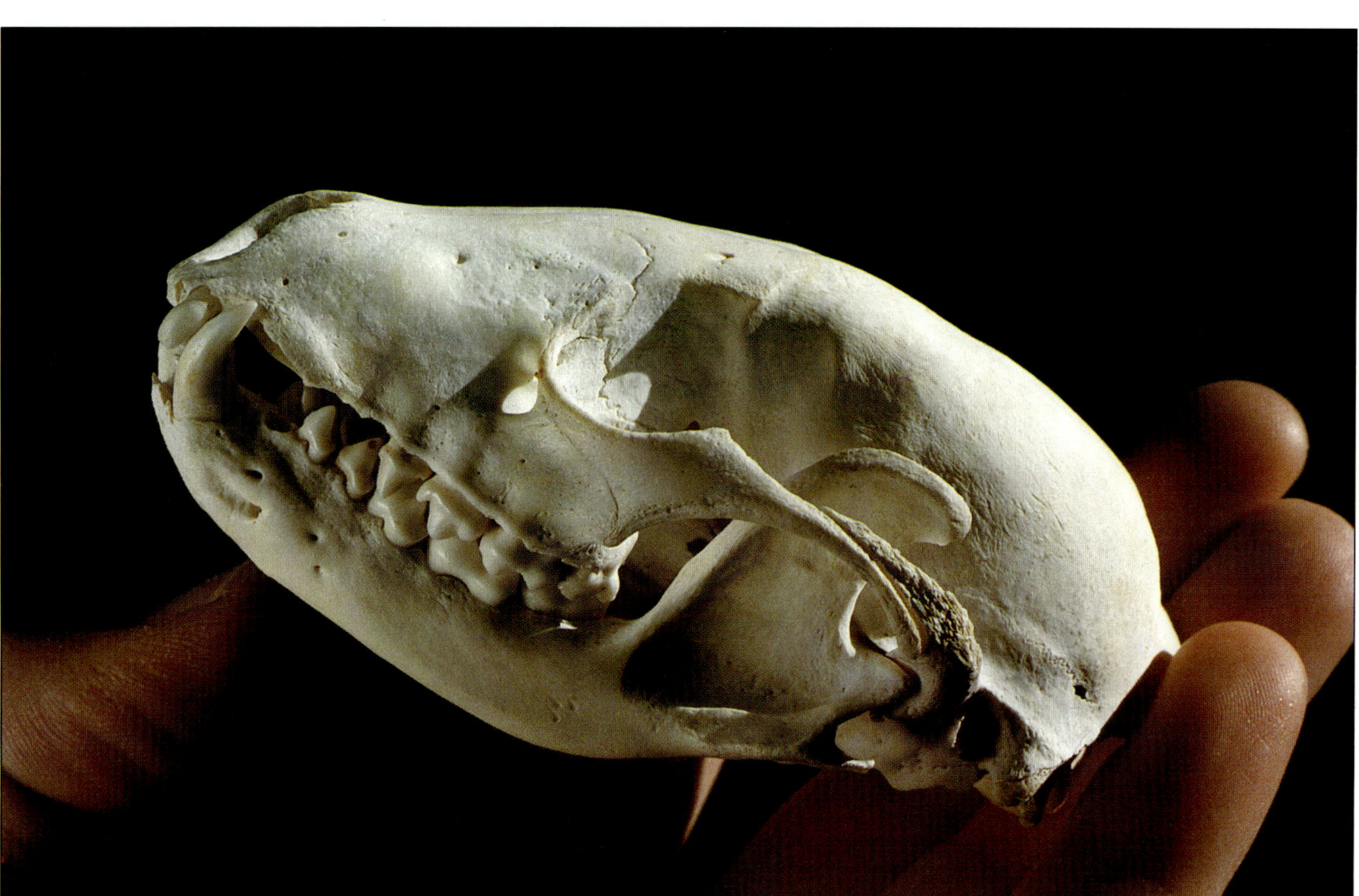

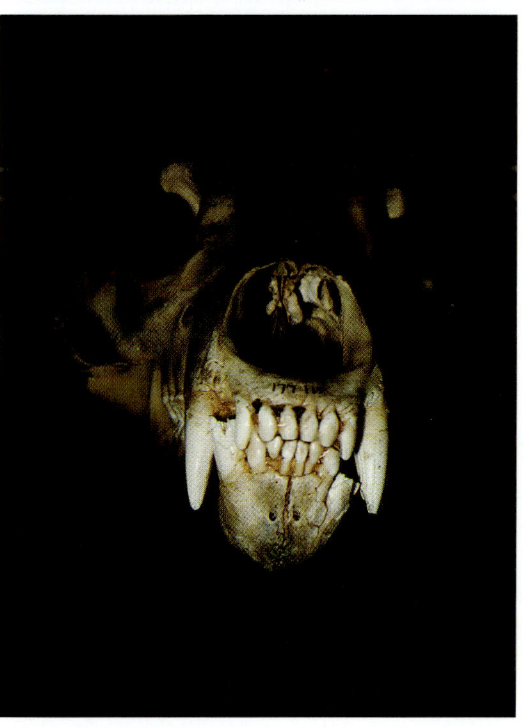

you can, dry the skull thoroughly, then place it in a colony of *Dermestes* beetles, the larvae of which feed on dried animal tissue; colonies are available through biological supply companies. This results in a very clean skull, and is the method most museums use. A cruder method in summer is to wrap the skull in a sheet of wire hardware cloth, stake it down firmly (to prevent scavengers from taking it away) and cover it with leaves and soil. Carrion beetles and other decomposers will clean the skull over the course of several weeks.

When the skull is completely free of flesh, wash it well. To remove stains, immerse the skull in a dilute solution of chlorine bleach (one part bleach to five parts water) for several minutes – no longer, since the bleach can weaken bone joints. A brief soaking in hydrogen peroxide works almost as well, without damaging the skull.

ABOVE A raccoon skull, found half-buried in mud along a marsh, glistens after careful cleaning and a peroxide bath.

LEFT A museum's grizzly bear skull glowers from a display case; the specimen number is written on the skull in ink, negating the need for a label.

Appendix: Reference

EQUIPMENT SUPPLIERS

Carolina Biological Supply Co
Burlington, N.C. 27215

Ward's Natural Science Establishment
P.O. Box 92912
5100 W. Henrietta Rd.
Rochester N.Y. 14692-9012
or
11850 E. Florence Ave.
Santa Fe Springs, CA 96670-4490

Forestry Suppliers Inc.
205 W. Rankin St.
P.O. Box 8397
Jackson, Miss. 39284-8397

FIELD GUIDES

Natural history field guides are available for almost any area of interest. The oldest and most respected series are the Peterson Field Guides, with 37 pocket-sized volumes covering everything from birds and insects to wildflowers, minerals and the night sky. Peterson's *A Field Guide to the Birds* was the first true field guide, released in 1934. Golden Press also has a good field guide series, although not as extensive as the Peterson series. Other excellent bird field guides include *A Field Guide to the Birds of North America,* by the National Geographic Society, *Birds of North America,* Golden Press; and the three-volume *Audubon Society Master Guide to Birding,* Knopf.

RECORDINGS

In addition to helping you learn bird songs, owl calls on these recordings can be used for owling, and one unique record is invaluable for learning amphibian calls.

A Field Guide to Bird Songs (Eastern and Central North America); 1983.
A Field Guide to Bird Songs (Western); 1975.
Both sets complement the Peterson Field Guides, and are arranged in the same order.

National Geographic Society's Guide to Bird Sounds; 1985.
Contains 179 songs and calls, emphasizing confusing species in which sound is a critical means of identification. Not intended to be a comprehensive guide to all bird songs.

Songs of Eastern Birds
Songs of Western Birds
Common Bird Songs
Published by Dover, each tape contains 60 common bird songs.

Warblers; Borror and Dunn, 1985.
More than 300 calls, songs and flight notes from all 57 North American wood warblers.

Voices of the Night; Cornell University Library of Natural Sound, 1982. Sounds of 36 frogs and toads of the East.

BAT BOX PLANS

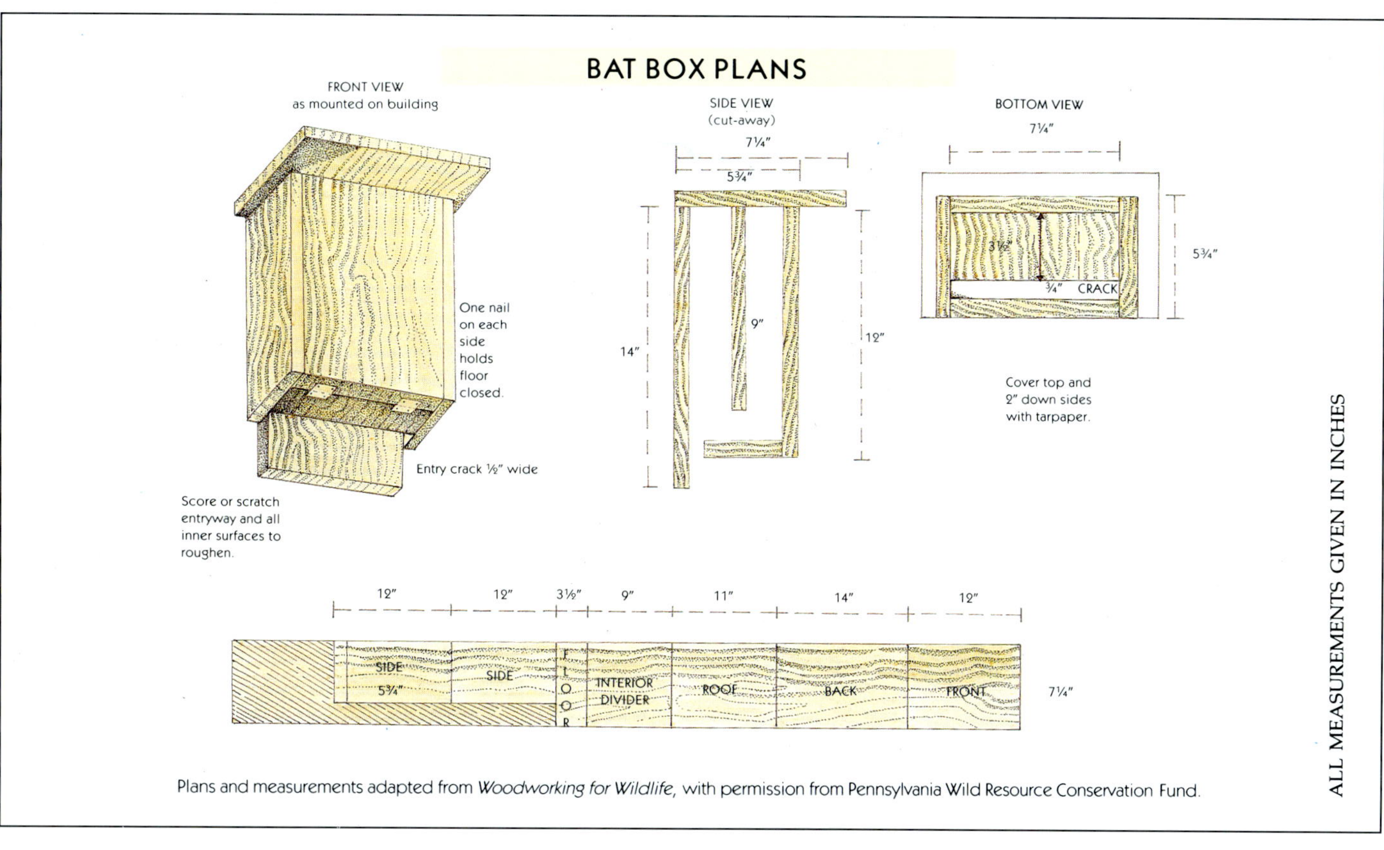

Plans and measurements adapted from *Woodworking for Wildlife*, with permission from Pennsylvania Wild Resource Conservation Fund.

ALL MEASUREMENTS GIVEN IN INCHES

TURTLE PLATFORM PLANS

(Plans and measurements for nest boxes, bat box and turtle platform adapted from *Woodworking for Wildlife*, with permission from Pennsylvania Wild Resource Conservation Fund.)

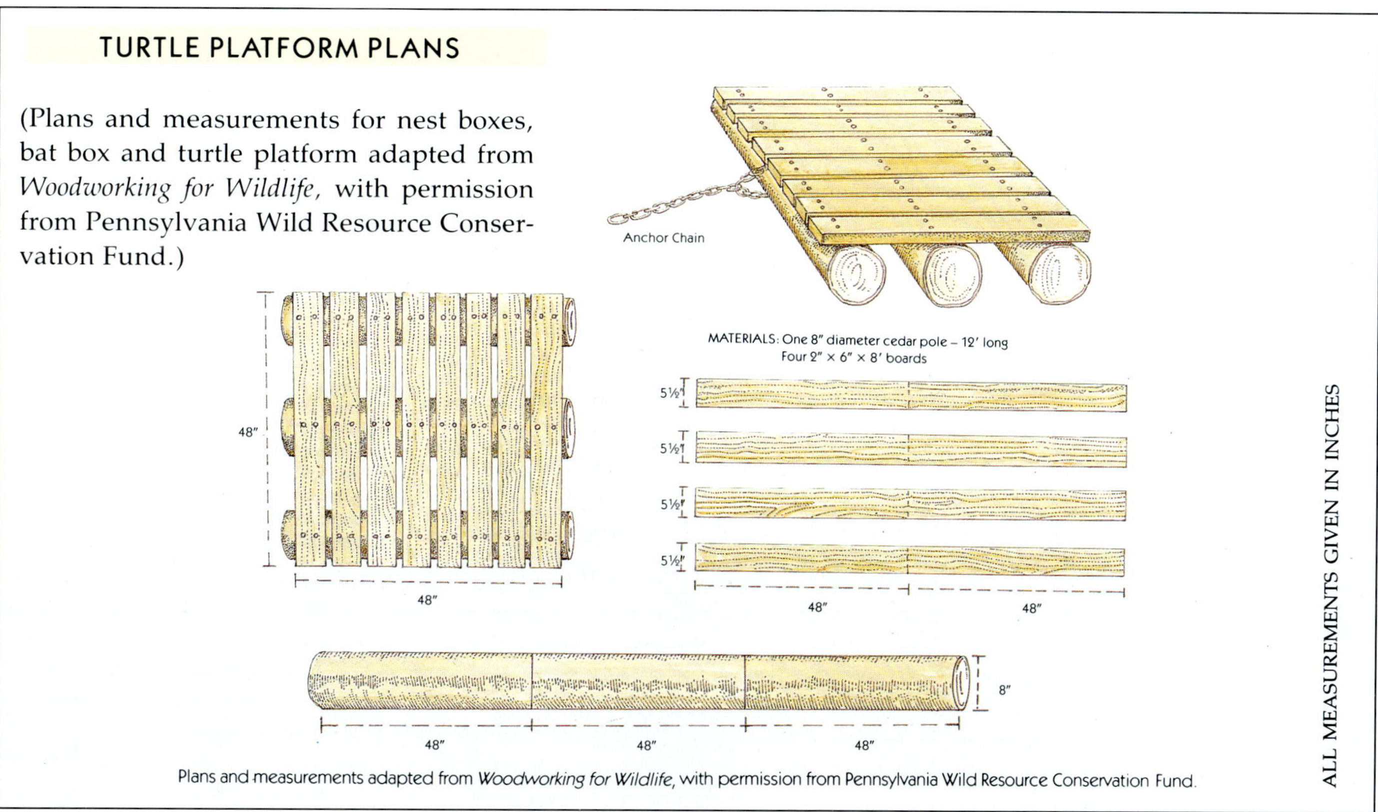

Plans and measurements adapted from *Woodworking for Wildlife*, with permission from Pennsylvania Wild Resource Conservation Fund.

ALL MEASUREMENTS GIVEN IN INCHES

Index